AFRICAN HISTORY & HOODOO

CONNECT TO THE ANCIENT SPIRIT OF AFRICA AND EXPLORE THE TIMELINE, CULTURE, ROOTS, SPELLS, & MORE FROM THE WORLD'S RICHEST CONTINENT

HISTORY BROUGHT ALIVE

© **Copyright 2022 - All rights reserved.**

The content contained within this book may not be reproduced, duplicated, or transmitted without direct written permission from the author or the publisher.

Under no circumstances will any blame or legal responsibility be held against the publisher, or author, for any damages, reparation, or monetary loss due to the information contained within this book, either directly or indirectly.

Legal Notice:

This book is copyright protected. It is only for personal use. You cannot amend, distribute, sell, use, quote, or paraphrase any part, or the content within this book, without the consent of the author or publisher.

Disclaimer Notice:

Please note the information contained within this document is for educational and entertainment purposes only. All effort has been executed to present accurate, up-to-date, reliable, complete information. No warranties of any kind are declared or implied. Readers acknowledge that the author is not engaged in the rendering of legal, financial, medical, or professional advice. The content within this book has been derived from various sources. Please consult a licensed professional before attempting any techniques outlined in this book.

By reading this document, the reader agrees that under no circumstances is the author responsible for any losses, direct or indirect, that are incurred as a result of the use of the information contained within this document, including, but not limited to, errors, omissions, or inaccuracies.

FREE BONUS FROM HBA: EBOOK BUNDLE

Greetings!

First of all, thank you for reading our books. As fellow passionate readers of History and Mythology, we aim to create the very best books for our readers.

Now, we invite you to join our VIP list. As a welcome gift, we offer the History & Mythology Ebook Bundle below for free. Plus you can be the first to receive new books and exclusives! Remember it's 100% free to join.

Simply scan the QR code to join.

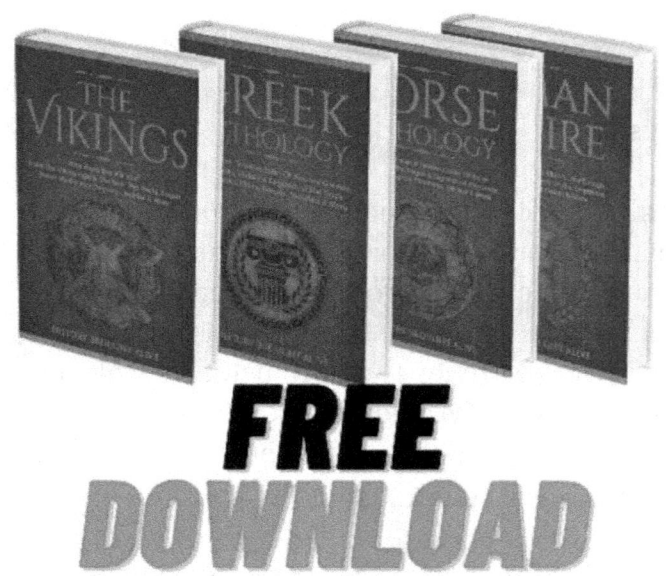

Keep up to date with us on:

YouTube: History Brought Alive

Facebook: History Brought Alive

www.historybroughtalive.com

CONTENTS

AFRICAN HISTORY: EXPLORING THE AMAZING TIMELINE OF THE WORLD'S RICHEST CONTINENT – THE HISTORY, CULTURE, FOLKLORE, MYTHOLOGY & MORE OF AFRICA

INTRODUCTION 1

CHAPTER 1: HOMO SAPIENS IN AFRICA 5

CHAPTER 2: THE SAN 9
    GROUPS AND POLITICAL SYSTEMS 9
    SPIRITUAL BELIEFS 11
    FOLKTALES 14
    LIFE, HABITS, AND FRIENDS 17

CHAPTER 3: THE HADZA 21
    GROUPS AND POLITICAL SYSTEMS 22
    SPIRITUAL BELIEFS 24
    FOLKTALES 24
    LIFE, HABITS, AND FRIENDS 26

CHAPTER 4: THE KHOI 29
    GROUPS AND POLITICAL SYSTEMS 30
    SPIRITUAL BELIEFS 31
    FOLKTALES 31
    LIFE, HABITS, AND FRIENDS 33

CHAPTER 5: PYGMY PEOPLE 39
    GROUPS AND POLITICAL SYSTEMS 40
    SPIRITUAL BELIEFS 42
    FOLKTALES 43
    LIFE, HABITS, AND FRIENDS 44
    THEIR VENTURE 47

CHAPTER 6: ISRAELITES IN AFRICA 51
    ANCIENT EGYPT 51
    KINGDOM OF KUSH 53
    CARTHAGE 53

CHAPTER 7: THE BANTU 55

THE GREAT BANTU MIGRATION AND THE KINGDOM OF ZIMBABWE 55
FOLKTALES 62
THE NGUNI, SHONA, VENDA AND TSWANA (KARANGA) MOVEMENTS 63
KINGDOM OF SOFALA 65

CHAPTER 8: SWAZILAND **67**
A HISTORY OF THE NGWANE PEOPLE 67
SPIRITUAL BELIEFS 70
CULTURE 71
FOLKTALES 72

CHAPTER 9: KHOISAN AND THE PORTUGUESE **75**

CHAPTER 10: THE KINGDOM OF ZWIDE **77**
A HISTORY OF THE NDWANDWE PEOPLE 77
SPIRITUAL BELIEFS 81
CULTURE 83
FOLKTALES 85
KHOISAN AND THE DUTCH 86

CHAPTER : ZULULAND **89**
A HISTORY 89
KHOISAN AND THE BRITISH 94

CHAPTER 12: THE HOUSE OF MPONDO **97**
A HISTORY 97
SPIRITUAL BELIEFS 103
CULTURE 105
FOLKTALES 107

CHAPTER 13: THEMBULAND **111**
A HISTORY 111

CHAPTER 14: XHOSALAND **115**
A HISTORY 115

CONCLUSION **117**

HODOO FOR BEGINNERS: CONNECT TO THE ANCIENT SPIRIT WORLD OF AFRICA & MANIFEST SUCCESS WITH SPELLS, ROOT MAGIC, CONJURING, HERBS, TRADITIONS, HISTORY & MORE

INTRODUCTION	**123**
CHAPTER 1: THE HISTORY OF HOODOO UNRAVELED	**127**
How it All Started, Vodou and Hoodoo? The Beginnings	129
CHAPTER 2: THE BIRTH OF HOODOO	**135**
The Three Elements of Hoodoo	147
CHAPTER 3: GETTING STARTED WITH HOODOO	**153**
How Does Hoodoo Work? Spirits, Places, and Tools	155
The Rules and Parameters of Hoodoo Conjure	158
Powerful Spirit Places	165
CHAPTER 4: MATERIAL USED IN HOODOO	**181**
Hoodoo Candles	181
CHAPTER 5: HOODOO SPELLS	**211**
Casting Spells in Hoodoo	212
CONCLUSIONS: THE MYTHS AND FACTS OF HOODOO	**229**
GLOSSARY	**232**
REFERENCES	**233**
OTHER BOOKS BY HISTORY BROUGHT ALIVE	**247**

AFRICAN HISTORY

EXPLORING THE AMAZING TIMELINE OF THE WORLD'S RICHEST CONTINENT – THE HISTORY, CULTURE, FOLKLORE, MYTHOLOGY & MORE OF AFRICA

HISTORY BROUGHT ALIVE

INTRODUCTION

In 1000 B.C.E, a San man lowered himself behind the bushes, turning his head quickly to his brother as he muttered a soft series of clicks. His hands gestured toward an Eland Cow grazing in the field afar, alone and unprotected. The brother replied, and a plan was formed between them. They hopped off to opposite sides of the field, prepared to chase the cow with the wind so that it wouldn't sense the danger waiting (Balyage, 2000).

The men got into position, and a voice chanted the opening of the hunt.

The brother raced out. His cries scared the cow, and it fled. An arrow zoomed through the air, and a sudden thud raged through the quiet morning as it pierced the beast's chest.

The San man sent up a silent thank you to Kaggan, the great God, for he himself must have enabled them to find such a feast. The meat would never be finished among the members of his own family, but perhaps his neighbors and their families would enjoy the sentiment; after all, were it not for their relatives in the east, they may not have eaten at all last month.

Every part of the beast would be used. If it couldn't be eaten, they would find a use for it. The hide would be turned into leather robes, and the bladder used to transport water.

He looked down at the ostrich egg strapped to his waist.

The hole on the edge suggested that its time had come to be used by his first wife in her jewelry making.

His eyes darted ahead, his brother's chants of thanks distracted him from his thoughts.

He started off toward him.

Suddenly, his pace was interrupted by the sound of angry, vengeful words he could not fully understand. However, the tone and few similarities in dialect were enough for him to have recognized that these people believed him and his brother to be thieves.

He moved quickly to try to stop the argument starting between his brother and the strangers, but he was not fast enough.

He felt the wind beat into him, knocking his breath out as his brother fell to the ground, a blow dealt to his head.

What he and his family would not uncover for thousands of years was that the people who took revenge on his brother were the long-lost children of two starstruck lovers. The first partner belonged to his own tribe, and the second to a great enemy. Little did the tribes know, they had both come from one parent.

How was it that twins would become enemies and birth children who would ultimately destroy them?

African History tells the most exquisite tales of woe and wonder. They are the breathtaking originals of stories you may recognize from your textbooks on Ancient Egypt, Rome, and Greece. Ancient Africa is where it all started. As the birthplace of the human species, it's only natural that Africa also gave rise to many of our languages, philosophies, myths, and legends.

History Brought Alive breaks into the most recent and unknown historical research around African history, to create a uniquely sincere and detailed timeline of events.

Using reliable resources managed by credible researchers, eyewitnesses, and aural keepers, History Brought Alive tells a true drama that will have you curling your toes in awe and anticipation.

While many texts are outdated, History Brought Alive uses recent material and new scientific evidence to solve mysteries that have been questioned for decades.

Great time and empathy have been put into providing an accurate telling of events. While many historical accounts can be seen as disjointed, History Brought Alive strives to provide a coherent and believable flow of events.

History Brought Alive writes from the perspective of the people of Africa in an attempt to protect and preserve history as they know it to be. For who would know it better?

This book relays a detailed account of how Ancient Africa was developed, starting with its very first inhabitants. The book takes on the difficult task of piecing together the pathways taken by Homo sapiens and in doing so, presents one of the most fully structured current presentations of Ancient Africa. The book encapsulates the newest findings by world-renowned archeologists into an exciting and riveting time capsule that will leave you feeling as though you are watching from over the shoulders of the first Bantu speakers as you journey with them through their migratory patterns, cry over their losses and marvel at the Kingdoms formed in their victories.

This book will change the way you view Ancient Africa.

Every account you know, every story you have ever been told, is only half the truth.

Ancient Africa might just be the greatest land ever known.

CHAPTER 1
HOMO SAPIENS IN AFRICA

In 1925, a black man working in a mine in Buxton, South Africa, wiped the hot sweat from his head. He shivered, his body reacting to the lime chemicals he had been submerged in for weeks (Tietz, 2018).

He stretched out his hands, and leaning his shovel in between his legs, he clapped away the dust that had resided on his fingers, painting them whiter than he had ever remembered seeing them before.

His wife would complain if she saw him like this and tell him to wash the grit out from his nails.

He would have if he had expected that he would catch less dirt on them.

Wondering for a moment if he and his daughter were alright back home at his village, he pulled his shoulders back and smacked his shovel back into the dirt, kicking the spade in deeper. Leaning into the handle, he reaped the earth from its grave.

His eyes grew wide and his chest tightened as the face of a small child stared back at him...

Perhaps showing this to the management might afford him a raise large enough to see his family over the weekend for the first time in months.

The Tuang child handed over to Raymond Dart became the first form of scientific evidence that humans were derived from apelike ancestors.

After the discovery, a series of diverging bone fragments were uncovered in the area now known as The Cradle of Humankind, the place our ancestors are believed to have congregated.

Africa was an abundant paradise of streams and animals and an agreeable climate in comparison to some of the harsher and colder landscapes of the time. Africa was the perfect place for creatures to explore and live. Africa, during Pangaea, was a place considered now to be, the Eden from the Bible.

These creatures grew, the stronger and wiser individuals being the last to survive during such intense times, governed by ever-present carnivores and environmental disturbances. These stronger and reasonably more intelligent individuals banded together and, over time, evolved to create a new species of hominid. The last of human ancestors is understood to be Homo sapiens, though, with today's research in genetics, it's not uncommon to hear of people having partial Neanderthal genes.

Despite the coalition of genetic makeup, the first evolutionary groups reported are the San and the Hadza who are believed to have lived approximately 20,000 years ago.

What happened to the rest?

There must have been so many Homo sapiens in Africa, how could there only be two groups that were documented?

Africa has a rich and fascinating history that is difficult to translate into a set timeline. Exactly how, when, and where the groups recognized in society today came to be, we may never know. But the most common consensus is that Homo sapiens, who emerged approximately 200,000 years ago, evolved in Africa from Homo erectus, who emerged approximately 2 million years ago and then were struck by a heated change in the environment (Penn, 2019).

Where the land was once dry and pliable, it became soft, wet, and watery. Homo erectus tried to escape the clutches of their submerged environment but perished.

It is believed that Homo sapiens and Neanderthals lost their ancestors' more peaceful nature thanks to the growth of their prefrontal cortexes, which heightened their cognition and made these newly evolved species more territorial and aggressive than those before them.

The last of Homo erectus was believed to have been found in the north of Africa, submerged in the aftermath of an earth collapse.

Homo erectus never made it out and became extinct one hundred thousand years ago.

Neanderthals and Homo sapiens never felt the need to migrate beyond Java. They were smarter, more organized, and more structured in their planning than Homo erectus. Their new, wet environment suited them fine.

Despite the similarities in their biology, Homo sapiens had a larger prefrontal cortex, making them more intelligent and violent than the Neanderthals.

Though the groups could presumably live in harmony as long as they remained out of one another's way, Homo sapiens possessed one significant ability beyond the rest that ultimately led to the fall of their companions. Homo sapiens possessed the ability to communicate with other groups. Neanderthals could only communicate about resources and things. Neanderthals understood family through memory and instinct; their amygdala and emotional processing sectors in their brains were large, but not large enough to lead them to destroy the Homo sapiens before they themselves were destroyed.

Homo sapiens conducted trade and gossip long before they evolved into the people we know and see today. Language was mainly a series of dialects understood by most Homo sapiens groups within close proximity.

This ability allowed them to talk about feeling threatened, ridiculed, or distasteful of the Neanderthals.

They captured, killed, fed off, and enslaved their ancestral sibling into extinction.

Soon after the fall of the Neanderthals, approximately 40,000 years ago, the land quaked, Pangaea began to separate further, and the environment mirrored its new location (McKie, 2009). Heat, unlike Homo sapiens, had ever known before, crept through the paradise they had once called home. Most of them left, moving eastward through Europe and toward Australia, curiosity, and dreams of an easier way of life pushing them on. The groups split after leaving Africa, chasing resources toward the places they would settle into and become what we know today.

Two significant groups stayed behind, growing and evolving into the first reported descendants of Homo sapiens. These were the Hadza and the San people. Both groups drifted through Africa, following the flow of resources. Both were hunter-gatherers at the time and would settle wherever their needs would take them.

CHAPTER 2
THE SAN

—⋙✦⋘—

The San and the Hadza, after thousands of years drifting through Africa, separate and unaware of each other's existence, found themselves meeting once again at the Great Lake around twenty thousand years ago. The Hadza preferred to find themselves along the north of the lake, while the San preferred the Southern parts. Though the two had originated from the same source, they found from time to time kinship in but one regard, their language.

The San and the Hadza communicated using a series of clicks, chatters, flicks of the tongue, and other explosions of the mouth and throat.

This was a complex language, where mouth position, click intensity and even tone were pivotal in communicating succinctly and meaningfully. Much like in any language, the San used verbs, nouns, adverbs, prepositions, and context when communicating, making their language one of the first complicated forms of language to be spoken.

Groups and Political Systems

The San people were originally hunter-gatherers, having no need for growing crops or raising livestock. These nomads would move wherever their resources would lead them. There was no hierarchical system and no one person who ruled them all. Instead, immediate families grouped together in a band,

and each member had equal say over the handling of issues and concerns. The bands, however, would each have a designated chief who would be held with the challenging responsibility of monitoring the usage of resources. The chief was by no means more important than the other members, nor could their opinions override those of opposing parties. Their sole purpose was to account for the resources collected. This individual was usually the eldest and most respected member of that band and could be male or female.

Bands would group themselves through loose family ties and general residency to alleviate the challenges of everyday living. As a larger group, the San would participate in a variety of projects together. On each project, there was a respected chief, not one who led them within the project, but one who had a particular affinity for it. Children, women, and non-San descendants could still be viewed as individuals with great knowledge that should be heard and taken into consideration in the greater group discussions.

One of the projects that they were engaged in was hunting, which was predominantly handled by the men, but women could participate too. Another was the gathering of seeds, berries, and plant-based foods. This task was mainly done by women, but men were allowed to participate. Throughout the tasks the San engaged in, there is little regard for gender differences, but rather, the bands focused on gender capability. Other tasks included healing, cooking, inventing, crafting, and teaching.

For the most part, the bands would live separately in their own caves and housing formations. When there were celebrations, marriage proposals, rituals, or battles, the bands would move in closer together. While each band spoke its own dialect of the ancient San language, they could also understand the dialects of the other bands.

As far back as can be traced, it has been found that the San lived in Southern Africa, mostly congregating around the Western Cape Coast, though it was not unheard of for the bands to stray further north.

Spiritual Beliefs

The San believed that there existed a Greater God, Kaggan, the cunning hero and trickster of creatures who created everything from the mountains on the horizon to the fish swimming through the stream. He is the creator of miracles, fortune, luck, rain, and glory. He could appear as anything, even an animal, though his favorite animal was believed to be the eland cow (which is actually an antelope).

In the beginning, Kaggan created darkness, which was called Ga. There were no stars, no moon, and no fields. Ga married a beacon of light who would soothe his clouds and bring light to the day. They moved to a quiet cave where they birthed three daughters, the Mountains, the Plains, and the Waters. Their three daughters loved to go outside the cave and dance. Their parents liked to watch them, as did Kaggan. One day, Kaggan appeared to them in the form of an antelope. Seeing the Antelope, the girls and their parents captured it and cut it into five pieces.

While they carried the meat home, Water, who held the head, noticed the eyes twitching.

"Why have you hurt me so?" the head said, staring at her. The girl screamed and tried to explain what she had seen to her family, but they all thought she was imagining things, after all, she had a habit of being a tad dramatic.

The head began to vibrate, and so did the other parts. Water screamed and screamed until her family complied and put the pieces down. The pieces cracked and creaked before flying back together. The skin stitched back up, and the bones straightened. Once complete, the Antelope rose and looked at the people who had butchered it.

Since that day, man would forever know the God that is Kaggan and be humbled by his power.

The people who had a greater understanding and connection with Kaggan were the healers. Healers were not particularly gifted individuals with a spiritual conquest or who had experienced an awakening of some sort; rather, the San preferred to have many healers. Anyone could become a healer, but the process involved many days of travel and much sacrifice. It was not easy. The healers, once anointed, would indulge in visions or patterns of thinking in which they would encounter psychic instances of illness or death in battle or accidents, even when the participant involved was hundreds of miles away.

Following their visions, the healers would host trance dances where they would attempt to see further, and/or heal the rest of the group. The healers would dance, stomping their feet and clapping their hands to a beat as they twirled around in the landscape they called home. The other members would sing and chant, and when ready, would join in. Their trance dances would last anywhere from an hour to several hours, often resulting in slight seizures or episodes. Once started in one individual, the seizures would begin to travel from person to person, healing the individuals who participated and allowing the healers to restore both mental and physical health in the group and see the context of their strife.

If you happened to stroll upon such a sensitive and private occasion, your heart might begin to beat rapidly in time with the rhythms, and your body might sweat as you stared into the glazed eyes of the locals, healing their own through the passion of entertainment and spirit.

Along with Kaggan, they recognized his godly brother, Kagara. Kagara was evil and cold, and he was often found to consort with the dead. He brought disease, famine, drought, and pain among the living as he conspired with the souls of the dead to bring the living down into the darkness with them.

The dead were a jealous and hateful group. They weren't forgiving and kind, even if they had been in life.

The San were so afraid of the dead that should a family member or friend pass, the band would move, never to set foot over the area again. They believed that the souls of the dead remained there, independent and easily offended. Walking over a known grave was a feared task taken on only by those outside the clan.

Most San buried their dead and marked the grave. Even if a band didn't know the soul that had passed, they would have to be richly tempted before they would dare insult them by disturbing their rest.

Interestingly, although the San feared the dead, they did not fear death, nor did they harbor resentment for it. It was not uncommon for a mother to birth a child in the coldest of winter when resources were limited and force the breath to leave the baby before burying it shortly after birth. That isn't to say that they didn't grieve their losses but rather, that those losses were expected.

The same applied to new life. There was little festivity over the birth of a child and often pregnant mothers, along with a significant other, would retreat into a private space to birth the child before returning and reuniting with the family. There was no spectacle, baby shower, or large celebration.

The San often spoke about their acceptance of the inevitability of life and death, weaving these philosophies into their artwork and storytelling.

Folktales
The Musical Child

One such story told around the campfire went as follows:

Once, there was a Lynx, whose beauty was beyond comparison. As a child, alone and stranded, she met the Anteater. The Anteater's heart melted upon meeting the beautiful, sweet child and decided to take her and raise the Lynx as her own since the Lynx had not a soul in the world.

As the Lynx grew, the Anteater became aware that her child's beauty caused much stir among the other creatures. She gifted the Lynx a small guitar so that the threats surrounding her babe would become too distracted by the music she played to revel in her beauty.

The Lynx played every day at daybreak and every night at the sunset. Her song became the alarm for many in the area, including her mother, the Anteater.

One night, the Anteater noticed a rumbling in the earth, but thought nothing of it, for who would be so rude as to ignore her child's song while it played?

She went to sleep to the sound of her child's music.

A sudden sharp twang of her child's guitar stirred her in the night.

"Why do you play your guitar now?" she asked the Lynx.

"It wasn't me," the Lynx replied.

"How then could your Guitar play?"

"Perhaps it was a stick that had fallen," the Lynx suggested, for the two lived burrowed underground, and it was not uncommon for the earth to shift around them when there were travelers.

With her mind settled, the Anteater fell back asleep.

While she slept, humans came and stole the Lynx from her home.

When the Anteater woke and realized her child had gone, she quickly ran to the place where her baby had been asleep.

She felt the ground and noticed how soft it was. The ground was supposed to be hard. If the ground was soft, that meant that there was an air pocket somewhere.

She lay very still and felt the ground quiver with the footsteps of the people who had taken her child.

The air pocket was connected to the surface on which they walked. If she were to break into the air pocket and then the ground below, she could break the surface on which the people walked.

Using her large claws, she dug deep into the ground.

Sure enough, the unsuspecting victims fell into a deep hole in the earth, and the Anteater raced to collect her child.

Upon her arrival, the Anteater told her babe, "Did you not know that anyone who took you from me would crumble into the earth and die?"

This story showcases the love a mother has for her child as well as the intrinsic adoration the San people held toward children, even those who were not their own. The San loved children, and even as adults, tried to keep the childlike wonder of life in their mind's eye (Lewis-Williams, 2018).

The Springbuck's Daughter

Another such tale uses the same characters but places them under different circumstances.

One day, the Anteater goes out and steals the Springbuck's daughter, to raise and love as her own. She takes the child to her underground camp, feeds, and cleans her.

The child's father finds out what has happened through the words of a gossiping partridge and sends his valued ally, the Lynx, to bring her home.

While the Anteater was out hunting, the Lynx stole the child back and returned her safely back to the arms of her father.

But the Lynx also knew of the Anteaters' powers in controlling the earth and returned to her camp and waited for her to return.

When the Anteater came home and found the child missing, she went to the spot where the child had laid and searched for the open air pockets.

Before she could deal the blow that would send the surface of the child's home crumbling, the Lynx came up behind her and hit her over the head with a club, killing her.

The change of personalities within the characters is evident in San's belief that Kaggan can be and come in many forms. It further divulges the San's love for children, while also warning that theft, jealousy, and revenge are not tolerated (Lewis-Williams, 2018).

In the case of such incidents involving these spiritual ailments, the healers would perform a trance dance to cleanse the group and release the harboring of such negativity, which was believed to bring illness and danger.

The Lightning Fight

This story begins with a young woman on her wedding day. After the ceremony, she returns to her husband's home, where she will spend the rest of her days with his family. She finds her husband to be unkind and finds comfort in escaping in her few moments of peace to be with her family. Her brother, unnerved by the hateful actions of his sister's husband, comes to rescue her and goads her husband into a fight. Perhaps it might have been an ordinary fight if both men hadn't been healers. The brother slams his fist into the husband's nose. Bleeding, the husband slams his hand into the ground, forcing lightning to shoot out at the brother from the sky. Dazed, the brother reaches behind him and, with the heat stirring inside him, flicks lightning back at the husband through the palm of his hand. Both men have been struck, and both have been wounded to the point of retreat. The husband went back to his camp, and with no one who loved him enough to tend to his wounds, he died. The sister and brother returned home, where their family healed them with herbs (Lewis-Williams, 2018).

This tale explores San's ideology of equality, that one who harms another may suffer repercussions. It also explores their belief in the supernatural as well as their need and appreciation for healers in their community.

Life, Habits, and Friends

The San were peaceful people without much greed or understanding of it. They lived their lives as they could, using whatever resources they came across. Where there was game to hunt, they would hunt it. Where there was grass to craft a bed, they would. The world was their oyster. This incredible gift of being able to master the Earth as they came to it, would also be their greatest downfall.

Before the arrival and creation of hybrid groups such as the Bantu, the Pygmies, and the Khoi, the San and their brother tribe, the Hazda, lived peacefully, opposite one another at the Great Lake. Both groups were hunter-gatherers and so would stray every so often from their humble locations, venturing out to witness what more their African continent had to offer. The San enjoyed migrating southward, while the brother tribe saw something more favorable lying to the north. Other sites aside, both groups had a place in Africa that they valued above all else, and for the San, that would be the territory of the Western Cape.

Given that Southern Africa was never particularly filled with fresh streams and lakes, it's no wonder that the San found comfort by the cape. Even today, the cape holds the freshest and most abundant forms of resources in the whole of Southern Africa. The San too, much like the modern locals, enjoyed the indigenous flora and fauna at the coast, hunting the brave antelope late into the night and stalking out the leopard before it stalked them.

To the San, the cape was home amongst many. All this would change upon their meeting with the new migrants—the Bantu.

The Bantu had a different way of life—one that none of the local tribes in Africa had experienced before. They were pastoralists, not hunters. They grew their own crops and protected their cattle with the utmost security. For the Bantu, their prized and protected game was spiritual. To the San, the land and the creatures on it belonged to no one, even if the presence of certain organisms, stemmed from the arrival of other parties. The San did not believe in income or valuables. They believed in survival above all else and, therefore, harbored and protected nothing other than their own people.

These differences in ideologies very quickly caused a spark to ignite between the two groups that would lead to plenty of battles and disagreements.

Though the feud between these two groups would remain lethal for years, the arguments were not without reward. As with any form of hatred, new conflicts are bound to arise somewhere—and they did.

The living circumstances between the San, their brother tribe, the Hadza, and the Bantu lead to the creation of various hybrid groups. The Pygmies, the Khoi, and varying merged Bantu tribes were some of the most well-documented groups to arise during this time of expanding civilization.

There must have been more, but, history does not account for the specific names of the groups that existed within these boundaries at this time. Though one can try and trace back the origins of languages in an attempt to pinpoint the specificities of the groups that lived at the Great Lake, it is by far a desperate attempt because of the amount of intermingling that occurred. There are so many similarities between the ancient African languages, and, these similarities can easily be identified in Indian and Asian languages as well. The contexts that they were created in are too lengthy and complex to present one language at one point in time. It's an impossible task, even in such a technologically advanced era as we live in now. Perhaps one day we will have those names and those intricate details, but for now, all anyone can account for are the broader ideologies.

Let it be understood before we navigate further through the ages and towards our current day and age that the Bantu were a collective group of peoples who spoke Afro-Asiatic languages. Among the Bantu were probably hundreds, if not thousands, of different groups of different skin colors, ideologies, and habits. Some of these groups already knew how to mine gold, while others had great relationships with dogs and horses. Some were the finest hunters the world had ever seen, and others had spent generations learning about and tracking the stars.

CHAPTER 3
THE HADZA

The Hadza, like many ancient African tribes, enjoyed storytelling. One such story tells of their beginnings. What's chilling is that the story reflects what scientists have confirmed today with regard to human evolution.

The story goes that there were once hairy, apelike creatures that roamed the earth called "The Ancient Ones." These creatures would hunt, kill and feed on animals without fire. Fire was not possible because of the earth's primitive state. There simply weren't enough tools to start one.

"After breathing in the blood of his feast, he would find a comfortable spot under a tree. He didn't sleep in a house because his environment didn't call for one. What good would a home do? What would be more comfortable than his spot right here?"

Years passed, and the Ancient Ones grew to become "The Intermediate Ones." The creatures were not as big as their predecessors and had no hair on their bodies. They could control fire and use it to cook food, warm their homes, and scare predators.

'The group had begun to notice how the animals avoided them. The animals didn't trust and lean toward the people as before. Instead, the animals raised their heads up, gathering in their surroundings, and once sensing a presence, would stalk the humans or run in the opposite direction. The group needed something to hide their smell, something that was as fast as the animals themselves. Dogs were seized and groomed to join them on hunts. They made for fine companions and bloodthirsty killers.

Finally, the group evolved into how we see them in relation to ancient Africa and their presence at the Great Lake. The "Recent Days" people had mastered the art of fire and lived their lives comfortably as hunter-gatherers. Their homes were reformed to cater to their belongings and special mementos. They had learned to craft containers for food, medicine, and beer. They had found solitude in their structure of living, working, and fending for themselves during the day while telling stories and gambling at night.

They had become inventors of note, laughing at the tradeoffs of close and foolish friends as they gave their belongings after having lost a bet. The rage of the loss never built for longer than 24, as the evening meal was always sure to alleviate such complications. They were never short on meat, for they had invented a precise bow technique and a deadly poison that they applied to the tip of their arrows. No beast would ever run too far from their plates again.

The Hadza of Ancient Africa grew beyond this scope to become the people that we know today, but how they did is more intrinsically remembered after their migration. It is from the years before that there is much myth and legend about them and their way of life, especially since much of the San had become under threat in the years leading up to the present day. Unlike the San, the Hadza hardly fell under the control of passersby (Madenge, 2021).

Groups and Political Systems

The Hadza didn't have a structured system, but rather,

each person had an equal vote within their immediate family when it came to making decisions. They rarely interacted with their neighbors but might meet for entertainment purposes, gossip, storytelling, eating, and dancing. They didn't celebrate marriages, funerals, birthdays, or engagements but did celebrate the coming of age for boys and girls.

The men predominantly hunted, and the women gathered, though it was not uncommon for the roles to be switched. When the landscape was dry and animals scarce, the men would forage alone, sometimes bringing back small animals they were able to hunt while out. In the months when the resources were more plentiful, the men would travel in pairs and spend many nights tracking games before returning home with a large bounty of meat.

When a boy completed his first successful hunt and brought back a meal of extensive size, he was considered a man.

Women would often forage in groups and were almost always accompanied by a man. They carried with them tools to start fires, sticks to accumulate honey and dig for roots, and baskets for berries and shrubs.

The Hadza were resourceful people and their diet would change greatly depending on the season, their location, and their members.

Governed by where they might find their next meal, the Hadza moved frequently, and as such, did not have many belongings. In the hot summer months, when rain was limited and vegetation scarce, they would not build homes but rather camp on the warm ground and move daily in search of food.

Where conflict arose between neighbors, one would simply move further away.

Life among the Hadza was primitive and challenging. The locals were often exposed to diseases, famine, and malnutrition. Very few children lived beyond the age of 15. When a person or child died, they may have been buried or left for the landscape to consume. The kin of the deceased would then leave that spot, never to return again.

Spiritual Beliefs

The Hadza followed no religion but considered themselves to be spiritual beings, and they believed in two greater beings. These beings were the Sun Goddess, who created the earth and all its creatures, and her husband, Haine, the God of the Moon.

The men celebrated the God of the Moon through a special ritual performed once a month on dark nights. The men danced in the darkness, calling on the ghosts of their ancestors. They reveled in the history and tales of the men who stood before them, depicting their victories and sacrifices.

The ritual, known as the Epeme dance, was believed to build kinship between the men and bring good hunting for the months to come.

The Goddess was equally celebrated during the day through general blessings and greetings among friends and families. Her name, Ishoko, was embedded in many phrases, and her creativity, patience, and loyalty are told in countless tales.

Folktales
The Giants
There are many folk tales about Ishoko and her creations.

One tells the story of a Giant who helped her husband, Haine. Haine gave the Giant endless control over the Hadza people as a gift to show his appreciation. But the Giant was cruel and unreasonable, forcing the Hadza people to work late into the night and eat foods that they didn't like. The Hadza people rebelled and moved away so that he could not control them. Angered, the Giant sent lions, previously known to be calm and peaceful creatures, to kill and eat all those that had ignored him. Again, the Hadza rebelled, fighting the carnivores that lunged at them. Still, it wasn't enough, and the Hadza had to seek help from neighboring tribes. In the dead of the night when the Giant could not see them, they formed a plan to trick him, and while his back was turned, they would shoot him with poisoned arrows. Their plan worked and, the people went back to living their lives free of restraints and orders.

However, it would seem that the Giant had not lived alone. He had brothers, and though his brothers had not the power to control the people as he had, they had the capacity for revenge.

Thus, a war began between the people and the Giants. The Giants were strong and large and could kill a man with just a flick of the wrist. But they were outnumbered and plagued by the same needs as their enemies. They, too, needed to sleep and eat and bathe. One night, once the two giants had gone to sleep, the Hadza and their neighbors came and killed them. Relief was once again restored among the tribe.

The Man-Eaters

Some of the Giants had found pleasure in feasting on the flesh of the Hadza people. Devastated that her creation had taken such a vile and evil turn, Ishoko appeared to the group of cannibals as a friendly snake. The Giants, not hungered by the appearance, as their favorite meal was to be found elsewhere, had no need to chase her from their home. While they slept, she bit them, and her venom sucked the flesh from their bones.

Seeing her creations so lifeless and limp before her, she found she could not remove them from the earth completely, so using their bones, she transformed them into leopards. The Man-Eaters were allowed to live out the rest of their days in this form, provided that they did not hurt humans unless they were provoked or wounded by one.

Life, Habits, and Friends

The Hadza, much like the San and much like all the ancient African tribes present at the Great Lake, spent countless hours practicing and perfecting their abilities to live in harmony with nature. Even if that relationship was not a concern in their everyday lives, these people did just that. From the moment they were born, from the early hours of the morning to the darkness of the night, these people practiced their languages, hunting abilities, and knowledge of birds and trees and star patterns.

Above all this, the Hadza are most renowned for their methods of collecting honey. For thousands of years, the Hadza had developed a relationship with the local Honey-Guides, a species of bird found in North Africa that feeds on bugs and bees. They would whistle a tune and the bird would fly down to greet them and lead them toward the nearest hive. The foragers would then light a small fire under the hive to smoke out the bees, and the bird would catch and feed on any stragglers that lingered behind.

Once the hive was clear, the foragers would hack the hive open and collect the honeycomb in their baskets to take home (Giama, 2016).

Living alongside creatures with a heartbeat was not the

only means that the Hadza had to survive. They had, through many years, accumulated knowledge of plants, herbs, and their uses.

One particularly useful plant was the desert rose. The Hadza would harvest the stems of the plant and cut them into tiny pieces. They would then boil the cut pieces in a clay pot filled with water and placed them over a fire. The sap would begin to leak out of the stems. They would then remove the plant material and boil the sap further until the liquid dried up, leaving a heavy poison deadly enough to kill a large animal.

The Hadza were capable of more than just herbal remedies and successful hunts, they were excellent shooters. From the age of three, young boys were given their first bow and arrow. From then on, they were expected to practice and play with their tools every day of their lives. As children, they were exceptional, without ever demanding that they be treated as such. They would grow into hunters with vicious accuracy, able to shoot a bird or baboon as it flung through the sky, exactly in the center of the head, every time. Their aim was their deadliest weapon (Lederle, 2014).

The Hadza not only had a good relationship with their environment, but their approach to conflict also put them in good stead with a number of neighboring tribes. Most notable is their relationship with the Isanzu, a Bantu tribe whom they encountered after the Great Bantu Migration.

The Hadza, like many clans, began to suffer the repercussions of climate change at the Great Lake and moved North along with many other local tribes.

After the move, once they had settled further north, the varying groups didn't seem to get in each other's way much at all. In fact, the Hadza came to depend on the local tribes to help mitigate the challenges of their lifestyle. They had a rather close relationship with a Bantu group known as the Isanzu. The Isanzu were pastoralists and had gained herding and farming knowledge from the communities living to the north of Africa when they had first migrated through Africa, years before they had even met the Hadza. Though the Hadza disliked the tediousness of farming, they appreciated the idea of keeping dogs.

The Hadza's relationship with the Isanzu was more than a source of ideas. There are a number of occasions when the Isanzu helped the Hadza through famines by giving them foods and herbs. One such tale of heroism tells the story of how an Isanzu man came into the Hadza lands and died under the conditions that he was met with. But even in death, his love for his neighbors was strong, so he rose from the grave and traveled back to his home, where he collected gifts of meat and honey which he gave to the Hadza, saving them from the plight he had suffered (Madenge, 2021).

Notably, the Hadza had few enemies, unlike their brother tribe, the San.

The Hadza legacy reigned strong with their way of life today, still reflective of their way of life back then.

CHAPTER 4
THE KHOI

The Khoi originated within the surroundings of the Great Lake, a creation that emerged from the mixing of the various clans that resided there. Following the great migration, the Khoi encountered the Bantu most frequently on their way North. Inspired by their pastoral way of life, the Khoi adopted these practices with the indigenous African goats and later, Eurasian cattle. Despite their knowledge of farming, the Khoi were greater herders than they were agriculturists and would often have to move around governing how ripe the land was. When the land became dry or used, the Khoi would move, returning only once the land had become abundant again.

For this reason, their housing structures were small and as easy to put up as they were to take down.

Their herds became a symbol of wealth, where they had once been food without a source of ownership. The Khoi wouldn't use their stock for meat but rather used them as a form of currency. Only on special occasions would the animals be consumed.

For the most part, the Khoi were exceptional hunters and would acquire their daily meat from their surrounding environment—but, the accuracy of their shots dwindled after the adaptations presented by the Bantu. The San and the

Hadza would soon become their superiors on the hunting ground. But with the Hadza being overtly friendly and hard to trample over, the San were an easy group to target when issues arose.

Groups and Political Systems

Because the Khoi had cattle and therefore, wealth, they had a caste system separating those who had funds and those who didn't. Like in today's society, the poor struggled through life, claiming work permitted by the rich in an attempt to feed and care for their families and increase their stance in society. The rich, on the other hand, found tradition in marrying and settling beside like-minded individuals and families in order to maintain rank within the caste system.

These beginnings also incorporated the usage and implementation of a chief who controlled and laid out the beliefs, rules, and systems his people would follow.

With any induction of singular leadership, there are bound to be disputes or disagreements so it wasn't uncommon for new systems to escape the clutches of an old society only to start a new one, based on the same principles but governed by different laws.

Such deviations left multiple chiefdoms within one area. The chiefs of each village would often host meetings where they would discuss the availability of resources and how to disperse them as well as any conflict that may have arisen between the different villages.

Despite their willingness to negotiate, the Khoi chiefs were only responsible for their own groups and couldn't always control the actions of the other chiefs and their villages. Thus, the negotiation was a matter of possibility, not regularity.

As with many of the Ancient African groups, the men were

hunters and the women were gatherers, except with the Khoi, this was a binding rule. Only the men could hunt, herd and participate in official council business and chiefly negotiations while the women were expected to tend to the homes, take care of the men and their children and forage for food.

Spiritual Beliefs

The Khoi believe in a good god who created Earth and all its creatures. His name was Goab. They also believed in a conflicting deity who controlled evil, sickness, war, and death. His name was Gaunab.

Goab was, at first, a simple plant. When that plant died, he returned as a rabbit. When the rabbit died, he returned as a watering hole, then a hill, then a beetle. He first became everything that once lived, and then, he became a man.

As a man, Goab was a noble chief. He fought Gaunab on many occasions. Sometimes, he was successful; other times, he and his people would perish. But Goab would return, rising from the dead, to seek the destroyer once more. In his last battle, he used thunder and lightning to defeat Gaunab, bringing long and heavy rains to his people. But the Destroyer was strong and quick and hurtled a large rock at Goab's knee, breaking it.

Goab lives in the sky, tortured by the pain in his leg. Though he cannot be on Earth, he still brings light with the moon in the darkness and rain for his people.

Gaunab still lives on, bringing death and illness to all mankind.

Folktales

The Khoi, like many Ancient African groups, loved to tell folk tales. Some of their stories are about the origins of the land and its creatures, while other tales are about their gods.

The Crane and Its Neck

Once there was a mother Dove who lived on top of a high rock with her small children. One day, a hungry and sly Jackal came past.

Seeing the Dove with her children so high up he said to her, "Give me one of your children, Dove."

The Dove refused, so the Jackal argued, "If you do not give me one, I will fly up there and kill you all."

Terrified, the Dove agreed and threw one of her babies down for the Jackal to take.

The next day, the Jackal returned, and again, the Dove gave up one of her children.

The Dove cried after the Jackal had left, catching the attention of the Crane.

"Why do you cry?" the Crane asked.

"The Jackal comes here every day for one of my children. If I refuse him, he shall fly up here and kill them all," she explained.

The Crane shook his head.

"You have been fooled, Jackals cannot fly."

With that, the Crane left.

The Jackal came back the next day and asked for one of the Dove's babies.

"The Crane said that you cannot fly. I will not give you any more," said the Dove.

Angered, the Jackal went to see the Crane and, creeping up behind him, cracked his neck.

To this day, the Crane has a crooked neck.

The Hare and Its Lip

After his death, Goab found sanctuary in the sky, where he could spend his days in silence, mourning his wounded knee. He sent word to the Moon to have a letter written and sent to the people. The Moon called upon the Hare, one of his greatest admirers, and tasked the Hare with writing the following:

"As I am dying and rising again, so too are you dying and rising again."

It was a simple letter, but the Hare, in its hurry, got confused and wrote:

"As I am dying and rising again, so too are you dying and not rising again."

The Hare delivered the message to the people and returned to the moon to tell of the expedition. The moon was very angry at the Hare's foolishness and slapped him in the face with a stick, splitting the hare's lip.

To this day, the hare has a split lip.

Life, Habits, and Friends

Since the Khoi and the Bantu shared similarities, the groups often got on rather well. This led to a mass expansion of mineral wealth owned by the Khoi such as copper and iron, all resources brought by the Bantu from their migration through Europe. Along with these, gold, beads, cloth, and oils were other commonly traded goods between the groups.

But if the groups had such great ties, what could lead the Bantu to chase the Khoi out of North Africa, all the way to the southern coast?

Multiple factors governed the systems that had to fall in

order for that to happen.

Firstly, the effect of climate change on the Khoi caused internal conflicts to stir. As their environment changed, the locals predicted that the rules would change with it, but they didn't, and many of the youth left to create clans of their own. This expanded the area that the Khoi were traversing remarkably and led to the settlement of Khoi in various Bantu states, some of which were accepting, and many of which were not.

The Khoi had always been a people who wanted to share their beliefs with the world and bring outsiders under their wings. The Bantu, equally proud people, confronted outsiders with the same outlook. This, mixed with the diminishing size of the various clans and the increasing level of disorganization within them, led to external conflicts, which the Khoi often could not defend themselves.

With resources dwindling because of the drying up of the environment, their expansion on one hand and their need to navigate into occupied territory to feed their livestock led to further confrontations that wouldn't have happened so quickly had the environment been tamer.

Hungry and ungoverned, the Khoi found themselves prey in a land that they once controlled. Those who hadn't been killed or swept up into other tribes through marriage or slavery, fled, settling in the South. This turbulent time led to the creation of a Bantu-Khoi combination group, the Korana.

The Korana

In the 1830s, the Korana was ruled by Gert Hooyman (Kora, n.d.). He led his people through the lands of a Bantu subgroup, the Ndebele tribe. During this time, the Ndebele were being ruled by the powerful Mzilikazi. While passing through, there was no sign of the fearsome army that had been reported by the neighboring tribes, and so the group fancied themselves content in the home of their enemies.

At the time, Mzilikazi was feared as much as he was respected. He had come from the Great Zulu Kingdom and had been a close companion of Shaka, King of the Zulus, a subbranch of the Bantus that chose to reside in central Africa after the Great Migration. The Bantus, like the Khoi, saw cattle as a form of wealth. Shaka would frequently send his warriors out to raid the lands for these precious creatures. One day, after a successful raid, Mzilikazi chose to go against his friend and keep all the cattle for himself. He left, taking his followers as far away from the Zulu Kingdom as he could, in fear of the retribution he might suffer. Once they had settled in the southern parts of Africa, Mzilikazi, like Shaka, raided the surrounding tribes and expanded his territory. His men grew strong and fought as valiant warriors do. Still, to those around them, they were seen as thieves, tricksters, and murderers. Most swore never to stand in their path.

Perhaps, though, it was all baseless rumor. Having come from the far north, Hooyman could not be sure if the tales told to him by prisoners of lost tribes were true or simply a means of distraction.

As they passed through the land, the Korana raided the cattle available, herding some and slaughtering others for meat. After all, unprotected cattle might as well have no value.

Together Hooyman and his people feasted on the meat, cooking and eating it in the clear and serene location once believed to be owned by true warriors.

While he feasted, two Ndebele women found him. Taken by his kindness and humor the women chose to warn him that he was not alone. Mzilikazi's great army was away raiding another tribe but the Ndebele elders were present and in hiding and would wait until he and his followers fell asleep to slaughter them.

Hooymen and his people scoured the land but it was completely empty.

Perhaps the women had tried to fool him into leaving? Perhaps they were afraid his people would harm them? Or perhaps they were hiding cattle elsewhere and didn't want him to find it.

Nonetheless, he couldn't see a reason not to stay, and with no sign of the great army's return, he and his people settled in for the night.

But, it would prove that the women truly had tried to warn him as in the depth of the Korana slumber, the veterans came and slaughtered them all.

Thousands of bodies lay on the once serene landscape, bloody and cold. Later, their skeletons would chill the bones of passersby, a deadly reminder of Mzilikazi's strength.

To this day, the place of the murder is called Moordkop and though no marking resides there to commemorate the Girque lost, they are remembered by those who managed to escape and later settle in Namibia and the Cape.

The San

The Khoi that remained independent channeled parallel to the Korana, both of them making their way to the cape. The Korana survivors of the Ndebele people met the last of the Khoi there. Together they were introduced to the San.

Though the groups first attempted to get along well, the San had a different way of life from the two groups. They were not herders, they were hunter-gatherers and to them, the land and its creatures were not something one could own. Seeing cattle in kraal meant little to them other than that their families would be fed and they wouldn't have to suffer organizing and following through on a hunt. This mindset shadowed their inevitable theft of the Korana and the Khoi crops and resources.

Angered, the Khoi and the Korana battled and trifled with the San people, pushing survivors further inland while incorporating the slow-legged among their own people. First, the San were used as slaves and traded between the two tribes. Over time, the San members were accepted in the community and given Khoi wives. Thus, the combination of the Korana, Khoi, and San peoples led to the formation of the Khoisan.

CHAPTER 5
PYGMY PEOPLE

Once upon a time, there was a father who had three sons, Katutsi, Kahutu, and Katwa. The father was ill and wanted to give his three sons a piece of his heritage before he passed. He decided he would delegate his belongings based on how responsible each of his children was and so, he came up with a test.

One night, he gave each of his sons full bottles of milk to take care of. When he woke in the morning, he found that Katutsi's bottle was full, Kahutu's bottle was half full, and Katwa's bottle was empty.

In recognition of the care taken to preserve the milk within the bottles, the father gifted Katutsi all his herds to use and enjoy for generations to come. Kahutu was gifted all of his seeds so that he and his future families could grow their own foods lastly, Katwa was given a forest where he and his family would have to hunt and forage for their meals.

That is how the Pygmy people view their beginnings, but the historical findings of how they originated is a far more saddening and delicate matter.

From the beginning of time, people have rejected individuals who were different. The Hadza and the San, like many groups, had individuals who looked and acted differently from the rest. These individuals were reasonably shorter in height and smaller in build. Their odd appearance meant that finding romantic companionship and marriage among those who were taller and stronger was difficult, if not impossible. These individuals, seen as the outcasts of their society, left if they weren't banished to live out their days in solitude.

Amazingly, it wasn't just one or two who got left out from their initial groups; rather, there were hundreds and thousands of these outcasts. This group of outcasts banded together, finding solitude in the quiet serenity of the forests, and became known as the Batwa people.

Groups and Political Systems

1000 B.C.E. entertained a variety of different forest life, and where there was forest, there was the Batwa (Kwekudee, 2013). The distance between these forestry locations, although vast, never led to much friction between the local groups. Throughout Africa, the differently located Batwa groups followed the same beliefs, religions, habits, and policies.

Batwa people, like the San and the Hadza, were hunter-gatherers. However, their smaller inhabitation, as forests, for the most part, were in comparison to dry land, didn't make them more accurate or valiant hunters than the taller surrounding tribespeople. They were hunter-gatherers of average skill and gentle-minded people who struggled immensely when taken out of their green homes.

A group of Batwa within a forest was subdivided into clans or families. The clans would settle close to one another, and participate in evening entertainment together, hunting, and marital debates, but, for the most part, the families lived and survived independently of one another.

The Batwa were mostly monogamous and, in comparison to their surrounding tribes, relied heavily on the authority of women when it came to managing households and everyday difficulties.

This is not to say that women in Batwa society had a higher standing than men. Men were still placed in positions of major authority, but the Batwa held the female identified in higher regard than that of other tribes.

For the Batwa, the women made many of the household decisions and often had a say in grouped clan meetings. This is because women mostly stayed behind at the settlement to fish and gather food while the men went off hunting. Thus, the time they spent at the settlement was more than the men and allowed for the women to have had a better understanding of the disputes that needed settling within these areas.

In addition, because the women were in close proximity to the homes during the day, they were expected to cook, clean, take care of and educate the children as well as managing household finances and clan resources. This made them pivotal in the Pygmy society and valued members when it came to decision-making.

The opinions of the women could be voiced during the council of elders, which was held every so often when domestic disputes became large enough to require mediation. The council of elders was built up of the oldest people within each family clan. A Chief, usually the oldest out of the gentlemen, would lead the discussions, enforcing that every person had equal say.

What was inherently sad, was that these pivotal members of Batwa society were often taken for granted by neighboring, unrelated tribesmen. The Batwa woman was frequently kidnapped and abused, leaving them and their families paralyzed and without a medium for decision-making.

Over time, these groups of beautiful people suffered great illnesses and strife at the hands of brutal neighbors, who even today, take advantage of the surviving peoples, hurt them and prolong their suffering.

Spiritual Beliefs

The Batwa had no religious belief systems. Rather, they worshiped the forest in which they lived, claiming the space as their parents and themselves as the children of the forest.

The Batwa learned many things from their green parents, such as ancient medicinal knowledge. It was the herbology and healing techniques that had even their greatest of enemies falling onto their knees for access to their great, life-saving skills. The Batwa were exceptional healers and helped the Egyptians using the plants found within their homelands.

For their medicines, creams, edibles, and inhalants, they commonly used roots, tree bark, a variety of plant matter, and items such as gorilla bones.

Their years of practice in herbology had given the Batwa people one item of trade that every surrounding tribe wanted. Where their enemies begged them for assistance, their friends, mostly found amongst Egyptians, were gifted this knowledge without hesitation.

Though it seemed only the Egyptians could see it, the Batwa truly were remarkable people, and when it came to saving the lives of others, they truly did seem to perform the impossible. With these abilities, it is no wonder that their enemies feared and despised them. How could anyone compete with a group that seemed to have the knowledge to bring back the dead?

Folktales
Cannibals

Tales of the Batwa people have been told for centuries, depicting the people as fantastical, cannibalistic people.

Why spread such rumors, especially when the Pygmies are some of the most peaceful and poorly treated people in Africa?

The rumors began thousands of years ago, after the Great Migration. The Pygmies' forests were filled with rerouting peoples, Khoi tribes, and Bantu groups. Each of these groups brought with them goods that could be used for trade.

The Batwa were not, at this point, scattered all over the continent. They resided in one area. Their skill for medicinal practices was yearned for by many who wanted to get the best deal that they could out of Batwa healers. The prices for the medicine were low and maintained by keeping trespassers out of that route.

Tradesmen would whisper words of horror and sacrilege to anyone who dared mention the Batwa name in the hopes that they would be too scared to go and look for the group. If there was no competition, the traders could continue to get more for what they were willing to give.

The Batwa were said to be cannibals who had a special place where they would fatten and rub down enemies and trespassers with herbs and oils. They would then cook their meat above a fire and invite the family of their meal to dine with them in a specific hut where they would be shoved, and held down in their seats while their loved ones were served whole on a silver dish. There was no way these victims could escape, for the pygmies had men everywhere, watching their every move. Their teeth were sharp, and their bodies were covered in holes dug by forks, making them look ten times more terrifying. There would be no confrontation or escape. There would only be tears and pain as the family was forced to dine with their captives, eating the bodies of those passed. After the meal, they would be taken to the special place where their loved ones had been. They would be chained and anointed, prepared for the next meal.

This farfetched tale is far from the truth, though there are elements of the story that ring true. But to understand what really happened, we need to trace a timeline of the Great Migration and all those whom the Batwa encountered. For it is in these tales of encounter that the bitter truth to this rumor can be uncovered.

Life, Habits, and Friends

As the Great Migration began, and the various groups began to flee from the ripening climate change toward new hopes and new locations, the Pygmies stayed. Their forest had hardly been tampered with. The sun was not bright enough to destroy the insides, and they never relied on the dwindling resources of the climate outside. They had found peace in their home and solitude away from the rejection and snubs from the other groups. Here, they had everything they needed.

Unfortunately, they also had everything the outsiders wanted.

The Bantu, the first known trespassers, entered the forests and saw the potential for farming, hunting, and a better, cooler life. Though they were further away from freshwater, the majority of their wealth being cattle, allowed them to easily transport refreshments to and from the drying lake. They had a wild game, grass for their livestock, and fertile land. There was just one problem.

The Batwa were hunter-gatherers. They didn't believe in

land ownership. The Batwa would often strike at the Bantu's cattle and the Bantu would seek retribution, often to devastating effects.

The Bantu, by this point, had a well-organized political system that was controlled by one person who could make and abandon rules to satisfy their beliefs and the needs of their people. There were no counter spokesmen to help rework violent thinking.

On most occasions, the chiefs would send out their warriors to kill the Batwa people.

The men would bring back trophies of their conquests, as was the trend in any successful raid, and the group would marvel at the strange appearance of the Pygmy people.

The Bantu groups started to see the Batwa people as subhuman.

Still, the Batwa fought back, with all the strength they could muster. This was not just their home. They were spiritually attached to their forests, claiming the land as kin. They were devastated and enraged by the Bantus' destruction of it to make way for farming settlements.

They would strike arrows in the Bantus' hearts, and the Bantus would club and hack at their flesh in return.

In the end, the small stature of the Batwa was no match for the Bantu. Those who happened to be just out of reach, cowardly while they watched their neighbors die. Others fled. The group split into four with participants traveling east, north, and south. Those who remained moved only a few miles west to make room for their new neighbors.

The bodies of the dead were mutilated and eaten. The Bantus' victories over the strange-looking people made them think that the Batwa held some kind of magic. They believed that by eating the flesh of the Batwa, they might grow strong and be cured of their ailments.

Those that had been captured were enslaved, and the families that remained offered up their youth for the same purpose in trade for peace.

And so began one of the very first accounts of slavery. The Bantu group that had invaded the area had come to own the Batwa people and their children. Should those children marry and give birth, those children would be owned by the Bantu.

As time went on and the now separate groups began to settle in their new locations, each of them began to adapt to the traditions of their neighbors. This group was called the Ngombe. The Ngombe began to hunt and cannibalize their own people, and in doing so, were banished from the clan lineage.

To this day, the Ngombe is widely represented as the Bantu people.

Their allegiance to the Bantu and betrayal of their own allowed them to escape the ruins of their once peaceful home. They moved south, settling alongside their old Batwa lineages as they tried to rekindle their once close relationship.

In many ways, the Ngombe was able to find forgiveness and friendship among their neighbors, though never again would they be considered brothers. Even today, they are held accountable for what they did. As if reminders from neighboring clans weren't enough, the Ngombe themselves shiver at their past and try not to speak of their gruesome history.

One might hope that over thousands of years, the

relationship between the Bantu and Batwa has improved. However, that is not the case. Rather, many pygmies are still enslaved to Bantu masters and ridiculed publicly by the Bantu people. Similarly, the Bantu are attacked and murdered by the Batwa.

For the rich on either side, a celebration is not joyous without the bloodshed of their enemies. Weddings, births, and funerals all dictate to an extent the killing of local enemies.

Their Venture

Once they had migrated out of their homes, the Batwa changed and adapted to the traditions of their neighboring tribes and their landscape, cultivating four distinct subgroups, each with their own way of speaking and their own philosophies around religion and origin.

Batwa in the South

The Batwa were the first to settle along the land now known as Rwanda. They made their home in the comfort of the forests that resided there, for that was how they were used to living. They gathered berries and honey and hunted the game that lived among them, and for some time, it felt as though their past would simply be just that, the past.

Except that the past has a nasty habit of repeating itself.

After a few hundred years, the Hutu and the Tutsi arrived on land that is now part of Rwanda. The Hutu were herders, while the Tutsi were agriculturalists. Neither of the groups found comfort in living in the forest, so they began to destroy any means of it that would prevent them from living in the ways that they were used to.

Soon, the Tutsis had developed a monarchy, stronger than any of the groups in the area. They began to rule over the land

and its inhabitants, including the Hutu and the Pygmies, whose value in the society began to dwindle. The Pygmies, as always, were placed at the bottom of the caste system. However, they had learned from their ancestors' mistakes and weren't willing to make the same mistake again. Though some were taken as slaves, many offered their services to the Tutsi king. They would work as spies, warriors, entertainers, and medicinal healers as well as tradesmen for the monarchy.

With the new influences that surrounded them, the Batwa's belief systems and religious practices changed. They came to believe that a supreme being called Imaana created all the earth and its creatures. He was a loving and humorous god who loved children and enjoyed games. In the beginning, Imaana blessed his people with immortality. However, he found his enemy, Death, was working against his people too often. Hating watching his creations rise from their graves over and over, Imaana sought to destroy Death. He warned the people to stay away and hide. But one old lady, unloved by her family with only her garden to warm her heart, left her hiding place to fetch vegetables. Death found her and hid under her skirt. Once the old lady had gone home, he killed her and swept through her village, causing chaos among the people.

All might have awoken the following day if it wasn't for the old lady's daughter, who despised her. The girl threw barrels of sand over the old woman's grave so that she might not leave her resting place.

The next day, the girl came back and poured more sand on the old lady's grave.

She hadn't noticed the effect she was having on the potency of immortality for those around her.

On the third day, she came back and discovered that there were no signs of movement. The old lady had been rested for eternity, and so, too, had the gift of immortality.

To this day, the people shy away from death, hiding in the forests and in small huts. When a family member dies, the relatives move and take special herbs to blind the ghost of the departed from sensing them and joining the family in their new home.

Imaana flew away into the sky, for he blamed himself for the loss the people had suffered. The only one he lets close to him is the chameleon, who sits high in the tree and radiates within Imaana's splendor.

Mbuti in the Eastern Congo

The Mbuti, like the other Batwa tribes, settled in the forests of Sudan and were granted just enough time to forget their strife before they were surrounded by Bantu villages. The Mbuti found themselves living a dual existence, one in which they followed the rules of their rulers and the village folk and partook in their traditions, and a second in which they remained the unchained, free folk of the forest.

The Mbuti very cleverly adapted to the Bantu way of life when they were in the open. They lived in more permanent huts where they selected a chief who would be responsible for negotiating disputes with the surrounding villages. The chief was usually an elder who got on well with those respective communities. However, once they entered the forests for rituals, celebrations, hunting, or general enjoyment, there was no chief, and the people reverted to an egalitarian society.

The same rules were applied with regard to arranged marriages forced by Bantu rulers. The couple would accept the instruction and enjoy a lavish feast sponsored by the ruler on their wedding day. However, once they returned to the forest, they were not wed, would not share a bed, and could love whom they desired.

The Mbuti never lost the spiritual awareness their ancestors shared with the forest and continued to claim the space as being both their maternal and paternal kin. To them, the forest would forever be a sacred place.

CHAPTER 6
ISRAELITES IN AFRICA

The Israelites started making their way into Africa by following the Nile river from Asia and through Egypt, all the way to North Africa, where they settled in Nubia. Here, the Israelites began to mix with the strains of Bantu that were beginning to flow through the same channel at about the same time. These combinations would create the first Egyptians

Ancient Egypt

The very first ruler of ancient Egypt was originally thought to be a pharaoh called Ro. However, recent excavations have shown that this translation may be wrong. Rather, the hieroglyphics translate the name as 'Big Mouth' or chief.

The first chief of ancient Egypt was succeeded by Ka, the first known pharaoh of the mystical land of Thinis, which was the capital of Lower Egypt.

Narmer succeeded Ka and had the goal of uniting Upper and Lower Egypt.

Narmer had a son called Menes, who succeeded him when he died. During Menes' reign, he started cultivating the origins of ancient Egyptian hieroglyphics and beliefs by creating the well-known ankh and the djed pillar symbols. These symbols revealed the ancient Egyptians' understanding of mortality and the afterlife. They believed that the spirit could enjoy two existences, one in the world of the living and one in the world of the dead.

Menes later conquered and claimed Memphis as the Egyptian capital. It would be the seat of the Egyptian government for the next several dynasties.

Hor Ahai was the next Pharaoh. He was named after Horus, the Egyptian god of the sky. Egyptian folklore has it that Horus was the son of Isis, who birthed him after she had received the butchered body parts of her philandering husband, Osiris. Seth, his brother, and his murderer—as well as the God of disorder—had drowned him after he learned that Osiris had had an affair with Seth's wife and their fellow sister, and left her pregnant with a child, who she called Anubis. Seth then chopped up Osiris' body and threw his penis into the water.

Egypt expanded dramatically during the 26 dynasties that would come. By that time, Pharaoh Psamtik the second would change the capital of ancient Egypt from Memphis to the Meroe Empire. The Meroe Empire was quickly reclaimed as the land of Kush.

Batwa in Egypt

The Egyptians first noticed these short, miraculous people to the south of the Nile and instantly took to them. They found something magical and wonderful about the way the Batwa people spoke, walked, and looked. To the Egyptians, the Batwa were a source of good luck and hope, and the Egyptians would regularly try to invite Batwa to Egyptian meetings and affairs. The Batwa and the Egyptians had a trusting friendship, with the Batwa being paid generous wages to work as advisors to the pharaohs. Finally, these amazing people had found a group who accepted them for who they were.

Kingdom of Kush

Kush was mostly ruled by powerful queens who were not only responsible for the people of Nubia but were responsible for the lives and ranks of their sons as they tried to push them atop the Egyptian throne. It is said that the land of Kush is where the Queen of Sheba ruled for a time before she met and dabbled in romance with Solomon, who produced her as an heir.

The Kingdom of Kush was later called the Aksumite Empire.

The very first queen of the Aksumite Empire was Shanakdakheto, who was appointed by her supposed son, Psamtic II. Shortly after their rise, they met and welcomed the Romans into their lands. The Romans, through trading with the Greeks, harped upon North Africa. Seeing the abundance of agriculture and life that sprouted from the ripe soils of the Nile, the Romans were eager to start trading with the locals.

The effects of the Romans on the Egyptians and the local Bantu tribes would be huge and last right up until modern times. During their encounters, the Romans tried to conquer Egypt many times.

Carthage

Carthage was a city and trading port built by the Canaanites as they fled from Yahweh and his followers after being declared sinners against the one true God. Carthage flourished with its close proximity to Israelite, Greek, and Roman traders. However, Rome was becoming increasingly powerful. Having seen Carthage's good relationships with so many other nations, the Egyptian land resources, and the 200 trading docks existing within, they decided to conquer it.

This led to the rise of the three Punic Wars in which Julius

Caesar tried desperately to colonize the capital. On his third attempt, he succeeded and laid claim to the once-proud trading station.

Queen Amanirenas was the ruler of the Aksumite Empire when the Romans finally achieved their goal and were looking to expand even further inland. With bravery and courage, she defended her people and set out on an attack in which she conquered the Romans that had taken control of Southern Egypt.

The Romans would retaliate for the next two years, progressively pushing Amanirenas and her people further inland. Amanrienas was not one to give up, but after years of fighting and having lost her husband and son to the Roman Empire, she grew tired and was eventually defeated.

The Romans could have ruled over Egypt but chose not to. The Egyptian way of life, the heat, and the terrain did not appeal to their habits or understanding. They were incapable of living there and growing weaker by the day, so they left.

CHAPTER 7
THE BANTU

The Bantu were a colorful semantic-speaking group of various ethnicities that entered Africa through Asian channels. Having come from a long lineage of Homo-Sapiens that traveled outside of Africa for a time, they brought with them a wealth of knowledge that the indigenous tribes didn't have. These behaviors and ways of life influenced the locals in a variety of ways. For one, the Bantu's political organizational systems were far more intense, guided, and yielded faster results than the systems within the local groups. This, along with their knowledge in farming and herding as well as combat, made the Bantu an exceptionally powerful force. They too followed the Nile river, progressively moving further inland toward where they would find, the Great Lake.

The Great Bantu Migration and the Kingdom of Zimbabwe

The four major subgroups of the Bantu speakers are the Venda, Nguni, and the Shangaan-Tsonga. After the temperatures began to rise at the Great Lake. The Shangaan-Tsonga moved south along the east coast of Central Africa, the Venda moved along with them but chose to take a more inland channel and the Nguni stayed in the center but moved south and were subsequently the first group to reach the Southern African border. These groups then spread out as they tried to find suitable land to farm and keep their cattle. This meant that the groups often bumped into one another. Such encounters had a way of molding the emergence of new groups and new hatred. Some myths suggest that the encounter between the Venda and the Nguni people created the Sotho-Tswana.

Mapungubwe

The first child born from the mixture between the Shongaan and the Nguni was Thobela. Once he had reached a ripe age, he chose to abandon his family lineage and begin his own dynasty. As the Shongaan and the Nguni moved on, he stayed behind with his followers, the Karanga, and began to build a kingdom known as Mapungubwe in Lesotho.

One day, the settlers found a shiny speck of dust on the surface of the earth. It glittered in the sun and made for fine jewelry and decorations. They found that heating this mineral over a fire would melt it down and make it more adaptable. They integrated this metal into their everyday lives. Only later would they learn that they had found gold.

It wasn't long before the Karanga was attacked and conquered by the Venda under King Shiriyadenga. The survivors that managed to escape moved west toward Botswana, where they built a similar kingdom called Khami.

Shiriyadenga ruled the dual tribes of the Venda and the Karanga with majestic grace, so much so that the people began to believe that his home was a sacred place, controlled and adorned by the ancestors. To speak ill about it would be disrespectful, as it would agitate the spirits.

Venda Culture and Spiritual Beliefs

For the Venda, spirits were everywhere. Spirits of the dead lingered long after one's passing, and the spirits of the cave and the water could bring about your doom as well as your greatest joys.

The Venda believed in many gods. The most powerful was the Rhaluvimba, a golden bird of light that brought lightning and thunder. Their second most powerful god was the Sacred Python, a mythical snake that lived beneath the water and controlled the water sprites and ancestral spirits that lived within. When the water rose high, the locals would quickly get to higher ground and leave the sick and old behind. This was because they believed that the Python was sending his sprites to take those souls to a new life under the water. It was merciful and kind to leave them to the fate of their God.

The locals took care to worship their gods correctly, and their gods responded with adoration, gifting the people with an abundance of crops such as coffee, tea, beans, peas, and wheat that they could farm. For meat, the people would kill their local birds, cattle, goats, and sheep.

Roles within the walls of Mapumgubwe were specific and unwavering. Women were to tend to the fields and take care of the children, while the men would take care of the poultry, hunting, herding, and politics.

The Year of Hunger
An old Venda folk tale goes like this:

The animals had been starving, and the baboons were the most hungry of all.

"What can we do?" they asked each other as they watched the humans eat and dance with great joy.

"We need to send someone very pretty to marry the king of those people; maybe then she can send us back some food."

At that moment, the beautiful young Unyamaleli walked past. Her family grabbed her and skinned her alive.

Cold and scared, she agreed to follow along with their plan. She would go to the village, seduce the king, and marry him. Then she would steal mielie from the homestead and leave some in a pot by the river for her family to eat.

She went to the village, and the king was taken by her beauty. They were married, and she began to steal the mielie for her family and leave it for them to eat.

She did this for some time until she feared that the other wives were getting suspicious, so she stopped.

"Look at her over there, so rich, plump, and happy. It is as if she has forgotten us." Her family said.

"We must teach her a lesson."

All the baboons in the family could play musical instruments, so they picked up their crafts and began to sing.

The king was so taken by the singing that he invited everyone to come and listen and watch the baboons perform.

Unyamaleli didn't want to join in as she recognized it was the voices of her estranged family.

The King told her to come and enjoy the performance because it was making everyone happy, so she was forced to watch.

Her family loomed closer and closer until they snatched back Unyamaleli's skin and threw her back into her old one.

"Oh my god," said the king. "I've been married to a baboon."

This folktale is a reminder of how the Venda families address issues in their households (A Venda Folktale, n.d.).

Khami

The Karanga rebuilt their empire in the Kingdom of Khami. Khami, in many ways, was similar to Mapungubwe, with fertile ground, a good water supply, mountains of gold, and abundant plant life for their cattle to enjoy.

Khami was built of stone, as was Mapungubwe, but pictures of Khami depict much stronger, thicker walls as if the Karanga at the time were nervous about another invasion.

They had every right to be, as not far from them lived a budding Shongaan clan known as the Rozvi. It wasn't long before the Rozvi attacked the Karanga people at Khami and claimed the kingdom for the Rozvi dynasty.

Karanga (Tswana) Culture and Spiritual Beliefs

The ancient Karanga were peaceful people. They believed that everything that they saw before them was cultivated by their ancestors. The earth was the back of their departed loved ones and was, therefore, very sacred and fragile. Taking the land and its creatures for granted was considered deeply taboo, as was the idea of war and bloodshed. They didn't believe that the earth was something that could be sold, owned, or kept.

"Have this land," a Karanga might say. But what they mean is, "I don't mind you staying here. It doesn't bother me, so long as the ancestors are happy, and my people are unharmed. I will reside here too. If I need, I may use this land as you may use mine. You may give this land to another, and I will still be here if it suits me and you and whomever you have given it to."

This understanding of the land would become a dangerous source of misunderstanding between the Karanga and ambitious African kings.

The Karanga aimed to live in harmony with their world so

much that certain behaviors and habits were considered taboo. One was not allowed to kill crocodiles, elephants, or leopards, or they would strike misfortune on themselves and their clans. People weren't allowed to fetch water with dirty clay pots; they had to wash them first, or the stream and the rivers would die. Moreover, certain plants and trees like the baobab were not to be cut down or harvested for their fruits or produce.

Monomotapa Empire

The Rozvi were the ruling clan within a great Shogaan empire called Monomotapa. The King, Changamira, was known to be brave, resourceful, and a good warrior. He planned to expand his reign as far as he could and in doing so, conquered Mapungubwe from Shiriyadenga and Khami from the Karanga and pulled them under his empire.

Shona Culture and Spiritual Beliefs

The Venda and the Tswana are both subgroups of the Shona people. The Shona believed in a supreme being who they called Mwari. Mwari was neither a male nor a female, rather it was a power that lived in the sky. Mwari created the earth and all its creatures for reasons of his own. He didn't like to discuss those reasons with anyone. It was considered rude to question why Mwari did the things he did. Though, for the most part, he had everyone's best interest at heart, sending rain when the people needed it and hope when it seemed lost.

Mwari was not always reachable, so the people would communicate with the ancestors of their departed loved ones and the spirits of the earth.

These spirits could bring good luck or bad, depending on which person was communicating with them and whether or not they were displeased or happy. Illness and death were believed to be the cause of witchcraft and angered spirits.

The Tribal healers had the best connection with these entities and hours of agonized herbal medicinal practice. The healers would throw bones to conjure the thoughts and ideas of the ancestors in order to make a prognosis and set about a remedy.

Then, they would make offerings to the spirits in the forms of food, beer, and meat to try and appease them and gather their interest in healing the sick.

The Shona, like many African groups, were organized through a system of certified male and female roles.

The Shona were polygamists, so the husband would live with the mother and child of his first wife and follow a visiting schedule between his other wives and families. The first wife was responsible for handling internal disputes, while the husband was responsible for training the young boys for fighting.

Kings were positioned through a line of descent, with the firstborn son of the first wife being the heir to the throne. Once the king had passed, the rightful heir would be claimed King and rule among his father's following, while his brothers would rule alongside him as separate chieftains. The king was a title given to the firstborn. But, the position came with the same responsibilities as any chieftaincy.

When a new king was born a group of young boys was sent to work for the new princely household. By the time the king came of age, the boys who once helped change the royal babe's diapers had become his respected counselors, older, wiser, and more knowledgeable about the king than even he might be. These counselors would group together regularly to try to find means of handling the disputes between the chieftains, often to no avail.

Folktales
Senseless Murder

A well-known folktale told by the Shona is the story about the Lion and the Hare...

One day, Lion asks the Hare if he will care for and feed his three children while he goes out hunting in strange forests. The hare agrees, so Lion goes.

While out hunting, Lion catches a bird and yells out for the Hare. The Hare's face pops up from far away.

"Here is some meat," yelled Lion, and he threw the meal to the Hare, who jumped up to grab it.

"Are my children alright?" Lion then asked.

"Yes," replied the hare, so the Lion continued on his way.

But the Hare was hungry, so he ate the bird.

The next day, Lion didn't catch anything, but at the end of the day, he still called out to the hare.

The hare's head popped up from far, far away.

"Are my children alright?" he asked.

"Yes," replied the hare, so Lion went on his way.

But the hare was very hungry, so he ate one of the cubs.

The third day, the Lion caught a snake and called out to Hare.

The Hare popped up from far, far, far away.

"Here is some meat for you," the Lion said and threw the meal to the Hare.

"Are my children alright?" he then asked.

"Yes," said the Hare, so Lion carried on with his hunt.

The Hare sighed at the small piece of meat he had been thrown.

That cub was so much meatier, he thought, so he ate the snake and one more cub.

The next day, the Lion didn't catch anything but still called out to the Hare.

The Hare popped up from far, far, far, far away.

"Are my children alright?" Lion asked.

"Yes," said the Hare, so Lion carried on with the hunt.

But the Hare had grown used to his meal and decided to eat the last cub.

When the Lion returned and found his children gone, he asked the Hare what had happened.

The Hare blamed the deaths of the Lion's children on the baboons, and thus started a series of senseless killings (Makaudze, 2013).

The Nguni, Shona, Venda and Tswana (Karanga) movements

Shortly after their encounter with the Venda and their growing Monomotapa empire, the Nguni made a race toward the Vaal River. But, it was too late, the Venda cultural and linguistic impact on their group had caused many conflicts within the group, and the Nguni's split in half with one staying behind and the other moving eastward toward Mozambique.

The Nguni found peace here for a little while before the conflict in the group drove them to split again. As one stayed behind in the Mozambique area, the other moved east, toward the coast, where they would encounter the Shona people.

Something sparked in these two groups, they got on well, so made companions of each other as they continued to move southward through the Lebombo mountains where they would settle in a beautiful and mystical land, called Embo.

What Embo was like and what occurred there to make the groups shift again is still a mystery.

The people of Embo moved southwards toward Swaziland, where they broke apart into three separate entities.

The Ngwane occupied Swaziland under Chief Sobhuza the first.

The Ndwandwe, the second group, moved back toward Embo and settled on the west along the Pongola borders, where they started to build the Kingdom of Zwide.

The third of the three Embo groups moved South. Conflict eventually split the group down the middle. The first of the two groups settled to the south of the Drakensberg Mountains and formed the Bele-Zizi people, while the other moved south, settling in the Transkei as the Mpondo people.

The second half of the Nguni group that had split away and halted in Mozambique, moved south toward Natal. It is here that the Mtethwa settled between the Mseleni and the Mhlatuzi Rivers, where they created the Dingiswayo Empire.

After a disagreement with his father, the Chief of the Mtetwa people, Chief Malendela rebelled and moved into Zululand where he began the Zulu Empire which would be ruled under Chief Chama, followed by his son, Senzangakhona and later, the greatest African leader of all time, Shaka Zulu.

The Nguni who had escaped the clutches of the Venda and had settled along the Vaal River moved south-east toward the Drakensberg where the Bele-Zizi had settled and established themselves as the Xhosa and the Thembu. The two groups passed through unscathed and settled alongside the Mpondo with the Xhosa placing themselves in the highlands.

Kingdom of Sofala

Shortly after the migrations from the Great Lake, the Arabs arrived and began trading their gold, copper, and spices with the now mixed Khoisan tribe. For the most part, the group was on good terms with the Khoisan, who helped them move farther inland and where they built a trading port.

A few years later, the group was joined by a subclan of the Karanga that was known as the Ghoya who also established good relations with the Arabs.

With the Khoi helping from time to time but residing happily in the cape, the Ghoya settled next to their new allies.

The Arabs, settling into their new home, found bounties of gold underground. They were as quick to pass on the word to their new friends and explain the minerals' relevance as they were to inform their friends outside of Africa, the Portuguese.

Mining stations and ports were developed with the Khoi and Ghoya working for the Arabs in return for gold and rich minerals.

A short while after settling, the combined Arab, Khoisan, and Ghoya friendship was put to the test when the intruding Karanga and Batonga people, descendants of the Shangaan-Tsonga people, attacked and conquered them.

The Portuguese, arriving on the scene a short while later, was dazed by the ongoing battles of medieval central Africa.

The Portuguese themselves were quickly swept up under King Changamira Ratvi's reign within the Monomotapa Empire.

As Changamira claimed ownership over the surrounding clans, so thus ended what was the Great Kingdom of Zimbabwe.

Changamira went on to establish good relations with the Venda, the Arabs, and the Portuguese, but the Ghora and the Karanga were enslaved.

With the industries of Portugal and Arabia expanding rapidly, the Ghora became valuable.

From the Portuguese, Changamira acquired fighting knowledge and a large mielie crop. From the Arabs, he procured fine silks, spices, and animals such as the Basenji dog.

Changamira's reign in the Kingdom of Sofala was quickly ended once the Portuguese decided that they wanted more.

CHAPTER 8
SWAZILAND

A History of the Ngwane People

The Ngwane People found unification in their home under the leadership of King Sobhuza In the early 1800s (Gillis, 1999). King Sobhuza's followers were not numerous, and alliances need to be built in order to keep out the Dingiswayo and Sotho raiders. King Sobhuza managed to form contracted alliances with the Dingiswayo empire by marrying the daughters of the Mthethwa chief, Dingiswayo, and the daughter of the Ndwandwe leader, Chief Zwide.

However, his alliance with the Ndwandwe people didn't last long as climate change forced the lakes in Africa to dry up. Without water, the Bantu groups were forced to migrate again. However, with such powerful empires in place and such strong homesteads, migration was difficult. Battles over land ownership were more fathomable than the prospects of migrating and having to convert to a hunter-gatherer lifestyle. And so began a raging war between the Dingiswayo, Zwide, and Swazi Kingdoms.

All conflicts between these three kingdoms might have been resolved more peacefully if the respective chiefs had desired to distribute what was left of the land evenly. This wasn't the case, and each chief had his own agenda to acquire more land and civilians than his comrades. Their dreams and aspirations outweighed their ties of kinship. A wife was not worth the prospect of everlasting fame.

The Zwide had thousands more people under their rule than the Ngwane had and thus, their army was ten times larger.

Sobhuza was left with a choice. Would he fight, knowing he and his kingdom would succumb to the forces of his enemies? Or would he give the Ndwandwe people what they wanted?

Sobhuza figured that the defeat of his people would be too high a price to pay for any battle and took a small sample of his following and left Swaziland. Those he left behind, acknowledged and accepted their place within the Zwide Kingdom. Even Sobhuza's brother restrained his reservations towards the new leadership.

One might have thought that King Sobhuza would have felt ashamed that the very beginning of his career had been met with his cowardly retreat. Instead, he was a man of incredible resilience and bravery. He didn't hide his face in shame. He handled his defeat with wisdom and pose. Following his retreat, he created a second kingdom.

His neighboring chiefdoms saw this and were drawn to his recovery, paying him tribute and creating alliances with him. This encouraged him to attempt to reclaim his homeland. He gathered a small force from his own followers and his alliances and moved toward the Dlomodlomo hills in the hopes of conquering more land and harnessing more allies.

Along the way, he and his people accidentally stumbled into the uncharted lands of the Sotho people, who kidnapped and imprisoned Sobhuza and his followers for many days.

That was until Sobhuza's charm won the alliance of the Sotho Chief, who eventually released Sobhuza and his people.

While Sobhuza was talking his way out of a difficult predicament and forming an unlikely friendship, Zwide's grasp on Sobhuza's lost kingdom was waning.

The Dingiswayo had started to attack the Zwide claimed lands more frequently, and Zwide had finally formed a plan to retaliate. He decided that he would take his warriors, and together, they would cross the Mahlatsi river and surprise their enemies on the other side, sending them to their tombs.

Zwide's plan may have worked if someone had not told the Dingiswayo chief of it. As Zwide and his warriors were crossing the river, the Dingiswayo warriors were waiting and with great accuracy threw their spears at Zwide and his force. Zwide and a few others managed to escape with a cowardly retreat. His life had been saved, but he had lost his empire.

As soon as Zwide ran, so too had Sobhuza's brother sent word to Sobhuza, begging him to come home and reclaim the land that would now be claimed by the Dingiswayo.

Along his route to reclaiming his kingdom, Sobhuza and his allies married many more daughters of great chiefs and had brave sons with them. Sobhuza's reign and control over the African lands grew until, eventually, he found himself in control of a large enough force that could enable him to reclaim his home.

As for the citizens of Sobhuza's lost kingdom, they had heard the tales of his growing greatness as well as his intentions to reclaim his kingdom. Now that Sobhuza had become so renowned, he was redeemed in the eyes of the people he had lost to Zwide's warriors so long ago.

While the respect for Sobhuza grew within his lost kingdom, the Dingiswayo chief felt it transgressive to fight against Sobhuza and his growing force over land that was so small in comparison to what he already had control over. Dingiswayo rallied his troops and left Sobhuza's old home, allowing the redeemed chief to step back into the borders of his once lost kingdom.

Sobhuza reclaimed his kingdom without bloodshed and when he did, the locals responded positively, paying tribute to him as their king.

As for the Dinganiswayo chief that had so kindly stepped aside, Sobhuza gave him two of his daughters to wed as a gift and an affirmation of peace. The two eventually became good friends (Gillis, 1999).

Spiritual Beliefs

The ancient Ngwane believed in a higher power called Mkhulumqanda. Mkhulumqanda created the earth and asked for nothing—no worship and no sacrifice in return. Mkhulumqanda is often very distant from the people and difficult to reach. Luckily, the women and the children of the tribe can see the ancestral spirits and ask them for guidance in the occasions that Mkhulumqanda's attention is needed but can't be obtained. It is the responsibility of the Swazi queen to make regular contact with the ancestral spirits to evoke the rains.

These ancestral spirits may appear to the queen and other women as ghosts, in dreams, or as snakes.

In the Swazi community, the inyanga and tinyanga are the healers of the group and the two people most closely associated with the spirits in the form of illnesses. The inyanga, using bone throwing methods, determines the ailment of the individual and suggests a prognosis. The tinyanga will then prepare a ritual and a herbal remedy that will alleviate the symptoms and or cure the patient.

The Swazis believe that everything around them is connected, and they work heavily with witchcraft and supernatural methods. On occasion, when a patient's illness is very serious, they may suggest human sacrifice as a means to a cure.

Along with the tribal healers is the sangoma who communicates with the spirits by allowing them to enter their own bodies. A sangoma is not a path that one can choose, rather it is a path that is chosen for you, a gift—or a curse, granted by the ancestors.

The powers of the young sangoma won't start to show until later on in life, and when they do, a choice needs to be made as to whether the individual wishes to pursue their gift. If they pursue it and do what they are destined for, they will live, but they must live their lives through the voices and words of their ancestors by allowing them into their own bodies. If they choose to refuse this gift, in a few months, they will die.

Culture

The Ngwane followed a hierarchical system based on the relationship clans had with the king and Queen.

The King and his wife were at the top of the pack, while their close friends and family, known as the King Bearers, were second from the top. Anyone who was not on a first-name basis with the King was placed at the bottom.

Once boys and girls reached a certain age, their families would begin to arrange marriages based on their place in society. Once the marriage was arranged, the husband would pay la bola for the bride in the form of cattle. A matrimony ceremony would be held, and the bride would then leave her clan to go and live with her husband's family until she became pregnant with their first child. By that point, the husband and wife would leave to build their own hut.

If the family was wealthy enough, the husband may arrange for a second wife. During the ceremony, the two women would be expected to look at each other and exchange vows as they accepted one another into their lives.

In some instances, the first wife would have majority control over the household happenings. However, should the second wife have a closer relationship with the king or the royal family, then she would take on the role of the first wife.

Within the city, the men were required to hunt and take care of the cattle, go to war and train the young boy in these areas while the women's roles were to maintain the resources of the house, care for the children, and harvest foods from the fields.

When a person dies, they are buried in the ground, however, if that person is of royalty, they are buried within a cave. The Swazi believe that once a person dies, they will come back in the form of an ancestor.

Folktales
The Flying Tortoise

The parrot flew down from the sky and landed on a branch beside her friend.

"Did you hear the news?" she asked.

"No," answered the bird.

"The cloud people have seen our drought and want to invite us all to a great feast so that we can eat," the parrot said.

"How kind of them."

The birds were the only creatures allowed to see the cloud gods.

The tortoise listening in on their conversation cried, "take me with you, I am starving."

"We can take you if you can fly," answered the birds.

"I can't fly," replied the tortoise.

"Well then, we can't take you with us."

"Please, I'll try anything," begged the tortoise.

And so the birds decided to help him. They went around gathering the feathers from all the other birds who had been invited to the feast.

The tortoise looked a little funny, but the idea worked, and he started to float. With a little practice, the tortoise flew with the birds up into the sky to meet the cloud gods for a feast.

"What will we tell them?" said the bird to the parrot. "They'll ask why he looks like this."

"We'll say he is the God of Everyone," suggested the parrot.

"Yes, yes, I like that. I am the God of Everyone, and my name is everyone!" Shouted the Tortoise, and they all agreed.

When they got to the feast, none of the winged creatures could believe how much food the cloud gods had prepared.

"Thank you for coming, everyone may now eat," they said.

And Tortoise lifted his head and ate everything, while the other birds could eat nothing.

The birds were so angry that they all took back their

feathers.

"Please, don't leave me here like this. I need to get home and I can't fly. I will have to jump, please leave me one feather?" begged the tortoise.

But none of the birds did.

The tortoise jumped and broke his shell on the rocks and from that day forth, whenever everyone sees the tortoise's shell, they remember what the cost of selfishness is.

This is a beautifully poetic tale that outlines the peaceful nature of the Swazi people (Hayzed, n.d.).

Chapter 9
KHOISAN AND THE PORTUGUESE

After having received word from the Arabs of a faster channel to India, the Portuguese started on their mission back from India and around the west African coast. When they arrived in the cape, they left their ship on boats and came to shore. Seeing life ripe and wealthy before them, they seized the women and the cattle they could and headed back to the ships.

The Khoisan men didn't hesitate to grab their weapons and with deadly accuracy shot the Portuguese thieves down with stones and poisoned arrows.

The survivors who managed to escape would be back for revenge for those who weren't and perished at the hands of the locals.

Three years later, as anticipated, the Portuguese came back and asked the Khoisan to help them unload a gift for them and their people. They handed the Khoisan an assemblage of ropes and had them lug the ship, and its prize closer to shore. Once all the Khoisan were lined up, and the ship was yet to reach the shallows, the Portuguese pulled out a cannon, lit the gunpowder, fired, and left.

Thus was the legacy they left upon the locals.

Over time, the Portuguese would come to dominate the trades of the helpful Arabs by destroying the routes and the ports the group had created, leaving many of them stranded and forcing further group combinations in Africa to take place that would inevitably lead to the Sudanese and Ethiopian empires in later years.

Hungry for more, the Portuguese became swept up in Africa's resources and, where trade wasn't possible, didn't hesitate to take slaves and raid lands for themselves.

Their ambitions led them to the Monomotapa Empire, where they noticed the squirming for power between the chieftains. The King at the time was tired and ill from all the interclan fighting. The Portuguese took advantage and slaughtered him and his followers, taking as many survivors as they could to sell as slaves. Thus, the Portuguese conquered the Monomotapa Empire.

The Portuguese continued to use the Kingdom of Sofala after their victory as a trading center until they conquered Mozambique, then the old dynasty became nothing but an old outpost.

CHAPTER 10
THE KINGDOM OF ZWIDE

A History of the Ndwandwe People

Zwide first began to rule over his people in the Kingdom of Zwide during a challenging and dark time. The heat brought on by climate change had dried the rains and the lakes, leaving his people thirsty and their cattle dead. The little rain that they did get was quickly sucked up by their dominant farming grain, the mielie. There was little to eat, his people had begun to starve and he was growing poor. It was a desperate time, not one for friends.

During this time, the two biggest Kingdoms in the area were Zwide and Dingiswayo. The Kingdom of Swaziland was massively small in comparison and of no significance to King Zwide.

He didn't think that it would be possible for such a small group to become such a big problem for him, not in the beginning at least.

And so, Ndinginisiwayo and Zwide began fighting over what remained of the river that separated them. There was one problem, Zwide's friends, the Swazi, lived right in the center of the battlefield.

In the midst of repelling and toying with the enemy whenever they came to the lake for a drink, the Zwide would fire arrows from their bows. The Dingiswayo citizens would run away and then bring back their army to retaliate, and the Swazi would, more often than not, get caught in the crossfire.

In 1817, en route to attack the Dingiswayo, they were ambushed while crossing lake Mhlatsi. King Zwide barely managed to escape (Chief Dingiswayo. n.d.).

Zwide ran as far south as he could, swearing revenge on the man who had taken everything from him.

Along the way, he and his followers met a white man on horseback. Although Zwide was unable to speak the man's language, he was able to identify that the man was on his way to the southern coast. Zwide and his followers walked with the man for some time and became increasingly anxious about him and the silver weapon he held in his belt. Zwide plotted to kill the man, in anticipation of conflict. Zwide reached for his spear, and as he did, the man pulled out his gun and shot, two times in the air, warning the people to stay back.

One of Zwide's men was able to spear the man from behind. The blade entered his heart and he fell off his horse and died.

That night, Zwide and his followers ate the horse and discussed the use of the strange metal weapon, and decided to use it to strike fear into the hearts of the smaller tribes that they might pass, and force them to join their group.

The next day, they continued south toward the coast, anticipating that there might be more of the white men there. As they went, they shot the white man's gun into the air, and nearly all the tribes they passed pledged their allegiance. Once again, his following had begun to grow.

Once they arrived at the southern coast, they met with the

Portuguese, who had just finished a trip to the Asian trading dock. They were celebrating, having finally found the fastest route to the trade center and, had happened upon this new land.

Zwide and his people, seeing the spices, clothes, and seeds that the Portuguese had, decided to trade their cattle and their copper for the items in the hopes of ending their starvation and increasing their numbers.

Zwide's following grew, as did his relationship with the Portuguese.

Zwide told the Portuguese traders of his woes as they settled beside each other for a little while in the cape. The Portuguese analyzed his warriors before suggesting a few remedies to keep his warriors strong.

The recent circumcision of his warriors had been leaving them weak and pained. The warriors needed to be strong in mind and body. The grazing off of a piece of skin was leading them to failure.

Zwide agreed to stop the cutting at once.

The Portuguese trader further taught and trained Zwide and his warriors in battle, helping them correct their stances and enhance their stamina.

When Zwide left the Cape to return home, he knew he would exact his revenge on Dingiswayo, and he was right.

He returned home to find his land had been claimed by Dingiswayo and his new apprentice, Shaka Zulu. Without much warning or introduction, Zwide and his new followers attacked the unsuspecting tribe and kidnapped the chief. They took their prisoner back to their reclaimed lands and executed him.

Zwide's wife, Queen Ntombazi, a beloved sangoma, placed the ex-chief's head on a stick for all to see.

For Zwide, the plight against the Dingiswayo was over.

If only he had known that by ending one war, he would subsequently start another.

His victory was not enough for him, and he went on to destroy the Khumalo nation. The Khumalo nation had been formed under the dreaded Sotho-Tswana people, who had settled at their place of origin along the eastern coast. He murdered the royal family—everyone except the king Mzilikazi Khumalo, who managed to escape. Mzilikazi fled to the Zulu Kingdom where he met with Shaka to tell him of his encounter with Zwide.

Zwide's battle strategies had been relayed to his greatest enemy and placed him in a very vulnerable position.

And so the battle of Gqokli Hill began.

Zwide came with his forces to greet his rival. What he did not expect was for Shaka Zulu to have his own warriors, the Dingiswayo, and what was left of the Khumalo people on his side.

Still, Zwide and his people had been trained by the Portuguese, and there was little that could frighten them.

The groups slashed at each other, coating the ground in blood. Zwide and Shaka fought head to head with blood-curdling screams and hateful teeth gritting. Zwide ducked left while Shaka swung right, and while Shaka's head was turned, Zwide struck him with his spear.

Shaka's face reddened in anger. He was not a king who would die avenging someone he loved.

With a mighty battle cry, he spoke words of encouragement to his fellow warriors. He thrashed and lunged at Zwide, who was bewildered by this transformation into a dying man.

As Shaka's cries grew, so too did his troops' energy. One by one, the Zwide soldiers' throats were cut, and their bodies were impaled. Zwide, as he always did in the face of defeat, ran.

He ran to his once allied brother-in-law, Sobhuza. Zwide didn't know that Sobhuza was in cohorts with Shaka. Still fairly loyal to his brother-in-law, Sobhuza warned Zwide, and so Zwide carried on north, knowing that if stopped, he would be caught.

The warriors weren't people of polite and empty conversation. They skinned and burned the people of neighboring tribes to strike fear into their hearts and draw out the prisoner they sought (Bryant, 2010).

Finally, Zwide arrived in Tonga country, where he was given a final meal by the chief.

It wasn't long before Shaka's warriors showed up and executed him.

His wife, family, and all the people that lived within his borders were killed and had their ears and limbs chopped off and burned by Shaka's warriors.

Zwide's only living legacy was Swazi, protected by her loving Sobhuza (Maringozen, 2022).

Spiritual Beliefs

The Ndwandwe, Mthethwa, and the Zulus believed that there was a mystical land called Uthlanga. In this land grew a huge tree. One day, a seed from the tree dropped to the ground and sprouted a reed. This reed was Unkulunkulu, the god who would create every man, woman, creature, and child.

He would accomplish this upon the day that he grew too big for his stems. He shed his leaves and walked through the mystical garden, where he found other people growing in the reeds. He plucked them out, one by one. Then he found a special herb garden where he plucked out the medicine man and his dreams. He walked farther to a drier area where he plucked cattle, lions, lizards, and birds for his people to watch and eat.

Once every plant from the garden was harvested, he realized that the garden would not be big enough for his creations to enjoy. So, he grew mountains, plains, rivers, and oceans and sent his people out into the world.

One day, he decided to leave his beloved garden to visit his people, but he found that they were starving and tired. He taught them how to hunt, how to build fires, how to fish, and how to make medicine. Once the people understood and had remedied their health, he gave them and all the animals and plants names.

He watched his people work and dance and decided to send a message to them.

'You will live forever."

He gave the message to a lizard to deliver to the people.

But the Lizard was slow and Unkulunkulu grew impatient, thinking his people had abandoned him. Angered, he wrote another message.

'Death to all.'

He gave this to a faster lizard, wanting his people to know

that they had angered him.

The faster lizard happened to pass the slow lizard on its way and, got to the people first.

Thus, people are not immortal beings.

It is believed that when a person is made up of a body, a life force, a shadow or darkness, and a spirit or soul. Each of these is a separate entity that works for its own purposes.

So when a man dies, his life force exits his body. If he has had a negative impact on those around him and has not completed his life's mission, his soul will fade away, and he will fade into the darkness to become a burden or a curse upon his family. But if he has had a positive impact on those around him and has fulfilled his goals in life, his shadow will disappear, and he will live again as an ancestor.

Culture

The Mthethwa, Dwandwe, and Zulus are exceptionally creative people. Music and dance make up a good proportion of their daily lives. Often at work, the women may sing songs to pass the time. The men may write poems or tell folktales about their legacy, dynasty, and chiefs. Their evening entertainment often consists of singing and dancing along to past battles performed by clan members while drinking pure, traditional African beer.

When they are not entertaining themselves with their cultural activities, the men are out hunting or training as warriors. The royals discuss political issues with their friends and confidants, but ultimately, they alone are the decision-makers, and they alone are responsible for their people's survival.

All fight training and hunting are first practiced with

sticks. Boys from the age of three are given sticks to beat each other with. Every day, they use them and practice, sometimes with mentors and sometimes without. The boys become rapidly strong swordsmen and as they do, they also become more attractive to the women.

On the other hand, the women's jobs are to harvest and plant the crops, manage the resources, make the beer, and take care of household funds. Though women are usually not needed within the politics of everyday life, their voices are strongest and most decisive in their own households. For it is they who care for the children, educate the girls, and make sure the boys don't kill one another while their mentors are hunting. It is therefore the women who know best how to handle interclan conflict.

As the groups grew larger, sometimes too large for the chief to maintain regular control, policing systems were put into place, and the chief would send warriors out to ensure that rules and regulations were being followed. The warriors would use their keen eyesight and quick awareness to quickly find where treason was hidden, and where they couldn't do any monitoring themselves, they would gather spies and allies to help them.

These groups were polygamous, especially among the royals and wealthier groups. While in some cases, status was determined by how close one was to the chief, in other instances, status was determined by how much cattle, crops, and metal minerals one owned.

In the cases of marriages, most were arranged, though later on, marrying for love became more common. Once a marriage was arranged, a payment called la bola would be paid to the bride-to-be's father before the wedding day and the bride would move to live with the groom's family after.

In many ways, these groups borrowed cultural and societal ideologies from their neighbors. Most of them were acquired after the rise of the great and powerful Shaka Zulu

Folktales
Why the Cheetah Has Tear Stains

Once there was a very lazy hunter. He sat in the cool morning watching a group of springbuck grazing on the grass.

How nice it would be to have some fresh meat and not have to do any of the work, he thought.

Suddenly he noticed something moving in the long grass. It was a cheetah. The cheetah was crouched low, seeking out a small springbuck. When the Cheetah was ready, she lurched and caught the springbuck. She then began to drag the meat back with her.

The hunter followed.

She carried the meat toward her den, where there were three cheetah pups.

How easy it would be to have a leopard do my hunting for me, thought the hunter.

And so he waited for the cheetah to leave before he went to the den and took all three pups.

When the Cheetah came back, she cried so loud that an old witch doctor walking past heard her. As the witch doctor learned of everything, he became very angry that the hunter had stolen the cheetah's pups, so he went to the village where he told the villagers the same thing. The villagers, too, were angry. So they all went to the hunter and kicked him out, rescuing the Cheetah's pups.

The old man gave the cheetah back her pups, and she was

very happy.

The moral of this Zulu story is that one should always treat the immediate environment with care and respect. One must also always hunt using their skills, and they must not be lazy (Zulu Folk Tales, n.d.).

Khoisan and the Dutch

During this time, the Dutch had entered the cape for the first time, wrecking their ship along the rocks. The shipwrecked men found sanctuary on the shores of Africa. These would become the first white people to inhabit the cape. After several months there, the group was finally able to return home on a Portuguese ship, where they explained the benefits of moving a colony to Africa. Not long after, Van Riebeck and his group of vessels came to do just that.

Their first encounter with the Khoisan was peaceful and resulted in an immediate trading post.

All seemed to go smoothly between the newcomers and the locals. Except that, very quickly, the Dutch's belongings began to go missing. Their slaves would disappear and be found hiding among the local tribes, and their cattle and their gardens would be depleted upon their coming home.

In revenge, the newcomers would take the Khoisan people and force them into slavery. The Dutch would butcher Khoisan clans and take their livestock.

The Khoisan would subsequently retaliate.

The relationship between the two deteriorated very quickly, and it wasn't long before the Dutch Embassy sent orders to Van Riebeck to remove the locals from their homes, and he complied.

Once the locals retreated, it wouldn't be long before the

Khoisan and the Xhosa would meet and combine forces to defeat the Dutch on several occasions.

CHAPTER 11
ZULULAND

A History

A young Senzagakhona was enjoying his days as King of the Zulus after his ancestor Malendellela had rebelled against his father, who had been the Chief of the Mthethwa people. Senzagakhona was a bit of a ladies' man, but even more so, he was a good chief.

One day, Nandi, a woman from one of his clans, proclaimed him to be the father of her child, whom she named Shaka, meaning beetle. He rejected the woman and denied the affair. Nandi and Shaka returned to their home, where they were also rejected on account of the chief. Nandi and Shaka left and wandered from tribe to tribe, trying to find a place to call home.

What man would love a woman shunned by the king? Who would marry her or even agree to?

Finally, as if the Unkulunkulu had a strange sense of humor, the mother and child found refuge with the Mthethwa people under Dingiswayo.

The chief of the Mthethwa was an expert warrior and a man hungry with ambition. He had his own ideas about warfare that had never before been attempted until his reign. He began to select his men carefully and then train them explicitly for combat.

One day, a leopard was seen sneaking into the cattle kraal. While the city folk ran for help and screamed for mercy, Shaka, who was eager to join the ranks of the warriors, single-handedly killed the leopard using nothing but his spear. While the beast leaped on him, he stabbed it through the heart.

This event gave him an idea. While he watched the Mthethwa warriors practice fighting by throwing spears back and forth every day, Shaka wondered what battles would be like if your opponent couldn't throw your own spear back at you.

He set off to design a new spear that could be used in the same way he had used to kill the leopard. He fastened a sharper and longer blade to a stick and called his intriguing invention the iklwa.

Dingiswayo hadn't been so ignorant as to not have noticed the boy's skills. After all, Shaka was the strange child who had offended his cousin. Dingiswayo had been keeping watch over the boy for a while, and with tension picking up among surrounding tribes, now was a good time to invest in the boy's skills.

Shaka joined the ranks and fought alongside the Dingiswayo warriors, and they defeated the Buthelezi, a neighboring Zulu tribe. Shaka had performed so well that he was immediately promoted. Following Dingiswayo's first defeat of the Ndwandwe and King Zwide, Shaka was given the rank of commander.

During their time together, Dingiswayo not only looked at Shaka as a student, but he began to see him as a son, wanting what was best for him and wanting to see him reach his goals and aspire to greatness that he was capable of.

Dingiswayo had defeated Ndwandwe and wanted to call a

truce with his cousin, Chief Senzagakhona of the Zulus. The two met and made amends, and Dingiswayo managed to convince Senzangakhona that Shaka was indeed his son. Finally, after a number of repeated meetings, Dingiswayo had secured Shaka's future: Senzagakhona had agreed to let Shaka rule as the next King of the Zulus after his death.

All would have been well if Senzagakhona had kept his promise, but he didn't. Instead, his eldest established son claimed the throne.

Devastated by the betrayal, Shaka could not be consoled.

Though no one knows why or how it happened, but, the new king was quickly assassinated.

Could Shaka have been behind it?

Though that still remains a mystery, Shaka and his mother took the throne, he as the new Zulu king and she, as the queen mother.

The two people who had once been shunned so intolerably had finally risen above all those who had shamed them.

Though he still held close ties with the Dingiswayo dynasty, Shaka began to build an independent military empire. Every man within his walls was trained in how to use the iklwa, and in time, Shaka had a group of 500 sharply trained men.

Still harboring the hate from his childhood, Shaka sent his warriors out to his mother's home tribe that had rejected them so many years ago. The warriors struck down civilians and children while Shaka and his mother smiled as they burnt the perpetrators of their pain.

This ferocious killing of all creatures without regard of age or gender made Shaka and his warriors one of the most feared groups in Africa.

All for Shaka had now been amended. He was content with his mentor and humbled by his mother. Everything was fine until the day Chief Zwide executed Dingiswayo and had his head placed on a stick.

Shaka's world went red, and he sought redemption and fiery revenge on Chief Zwide. Wherever the betrayer went, Shaka would find him.

Luckily for Shaka, he wasn't the only one who harbored hate for the Ndwandwe chief. Soon, Mzilikazi Khumalo approached him after Mzilikazi's home had been invaded and his family slaughtered. Together, along with what was left of the Mthethwa people, they banded together to fight against Zwide.

During the battle, Shaka was wounded, and though his troops were victorious, Zwide had escaped.

Determined to find him, Shaka sent his warriors out to look for Zwide with the instruction to torture and kill anyone who got in the way. Shortly after, Shaka's warriors brought back rumors that the King of Swaziland, Sobhuza, had been harboring Zwide.

Shaka, acknowledging that Sobhuza had never once harmed him and could be as hateful of Zwide as he was given the history, decided to make the man an offer he couldn't refuse. He would give Sobhuza a new wife and form an alliance with him, or if his gift was rejected, he would find a reason to get Sobhuza executed.

Sabhuza agreed but warned his brother-in-law about the danger ahead.

The warriors marched on, and no one has given mercy, not even the people of Swaziland.

They chopped limbs from bodies and ears from heads. They burned skin until it was crispier than burnt corn until, finally, they were able to track Zwide to a kraal in Tonga and executed him.

Many of the groups that had been tortured along the way had been forced under the control of Shaka and his Kingdom. Shaka had become drunk with power. He could have 50,000 men fighting for him for whatever he wanted at any given moment.

Then, in 1825, the British entered Africa (Flank, 2015). Their paths of destruction had been reported all over. Shaka had heard the news and feared what might happen if he was not on good terms with these strange people. He sent a group of his warriors down to the Cape to commence trading with them and cordially invited them to his lands.

Shaka had always been an eloquent speaker and a fast learner. Somehow, he was able to meet the British colonizers halfway and gave them the land and the people of Natal to do with as they pleased.

A few years later, Shaka's mother died of illness. Shaka was unbelievably devastated. Already suffering from mood swings and bouts of rage, he further lost his mind upon her death. As he mourned her, he forced his people to mourn her too. No crops were allowed to be grown or harvested, no meat was allowed to be hunted, no fish could be caught, and no celebrations were to take place. Anyone who broke the rules was punished immeasurably.

The people looked on at their once proud and heroic king in horror and pain. Their support waned, and the land trembled as the groups decided to start pulling away.

Something had to be done to protect such a great and pivotal empire.

Shaka's two half brothers, established sons of Senzangakhona, formed a pact and killed him.

As he lay dying in their arms, Shaka reportedly asked them to bury him in a tomb.

Thus ended the legacy that was Shaka Zulu's (Flank, L. 2015).

Khoisan and the British

After the war with Napoleon, Britain was a depleted nation. In desperate need of resources, they sent out valued members to colonize Africa. The group arrived on the coast of Port Elizabeth, where they moved further inland and began to establish towns around the Eastern Cape.

When the British arrived, the Dutch, the Xhosa, the Khoisan, and the Korana were already at war and had been for years. Siding with the Dutch, the British got involved and managed to hinder the Xhosa's movements into the coastal lands.

Meanwhile, both British and Dutch Missionaries had delved further inland toward the Zulu Kingdom in the hopes of converting the warriors to Christianity.

The rapid growth of the British colonies within the African coastal regions had chiefs rallying to catch their attention in an attempt to form a relationship that would protect them and their people from the tightening of colonist influence on the people. The African chiefs offered land, which led to a miscommunication in which the white settlers thought that anyone in Africa could offer land because to the British, land was wealth and wealth was property.

Once the lands promised had been seized, they would be taken again by a neighboring tribe or the tribe that sold it to them in the first place. This misunderstanding angered the colonists, who were quick to anger and ready to solve their problems.

Thus, without bargaining, the British, the Dutch, and various other parties began to seize the land of Africa, its peoples, and its ghosts as their own.

CHAPTER 12
THE HOUSE OF MPONDO

A History

After his father was killed in a war between the Bomvana and the Mpondo, Faku Ngqungqushe's brother was to claim the throne. But this didn't happen.

In Ancient Mpondo society, polygamy was a viable and customary way of life. Faku's father had married twelve wives and had over 20 sons. Traditionally, it is the first son of the first wife who will become the King's predecessor once he passes. If this doesn't happen, the second eldest son in the family is given the title.

None of this happened. Faku's mother was one of the later wives, and it was perceived that upon his birth, Faku would never have the title of chief.

However, when the time came for the new chief to rise, the council that advised and guided the chief found that none of the wives, except for one, was good, kindhearted, or eloquent enough to produce an heir that would sustain and grow the people.

After visiting their separate homes and dining with each of the wives, it was certain. The true mother of the people needed to be someone who could see a dispute from more than one side. She had to see people for who they were and discern how they felt without asking. She had to be smart—but not too smart—and giving—but not without hesitation. Most of all, she had to have sway over the previous king and the people. She had to speak so well that she made even deaf men hear. This was the mother of Faku.

Thus, Faku claimed the throne, unprepared and virtually illegitimate but very brave.

Tension swarmed throughout the family. Brothers swore against brothers as they tried to find peace with the decision of the Council, but as none of them were on the Council and as none of them were King, their concerns fell on deaf ears.

Faku's brother, Phakani, who was supposed to have been the late Ngqungqushe's predecessor left the tribe with his mother where they settled among the Hintsa Gcaleka, a Mpondo clan, hating Faku and his legacy from afar.

Though his other brothers remained, the resentment in the house was strong for some time. The elder brothers, Mtengwana and Gambushe, who were also close in line for the throne, were very angry with the outcome. Some sources claim that Faku and his two brothers went to war within the house, fighting one another with sticks to spears, hoping one another dead.

Eventually, Mtengwana settled with the Bomvana, the betrayers that had gone to war with his own tribe only a few months ago and killed his father.

Gambushe felt his presence would stir Faku into a frenzy that would inevitably lead to the younger brother's end, so Gambushe stayed and hoped that this would be the case.

Along with his family splitting apart to create tribes that wished for his end, Faku's beginnings were littered with threats from the surrounding Zulu influences and what would become known as the Mfecane wars—the battles between the Ndwandwe, Mthethwa, and the Zulu.

He didn't have much time to consider his new position before King Senzagakhona, Shaka Zulu's father, attacked his small home and its people in the Transkei. So quickly did the young King lose everything: his cattle, his family, and his friends.

The people saw Faku as a failure and ran to the Xesibe Chief of another Mpondo clan, begging for a new beginning, but the chief refused. One of his daughters had been married to the late Mpondo King, and he decided to keep his word to his late friend and ensure that the Mpondo clan remained sturdy. Threatening the people who had asked for sanctuary, the chief sent them all back.

With his people returning and his end nearing, Faku had to find a way to win back the respect of those who had rejected him. So he decided to start by seeking revenge on his father's killers, the Bomvana, now his brother Mtengwana's people.

This goal created further tension between Faku and his brother Gambushe, who had stayed. Faku rose three ranks, claimed himself as the rightful chief, and forced Gamushe and his followers to help him. Reluctantly, Gambushe agreed. Together, they raided the lands around them, moving through Hintsa Gcaleka kingdom, where Phakani and his mother had settled. They continued to be victorious, claiming back all the groups that had rejected Faku's legacy.

The Bomvana, with a new enemy and a chief with years of experience, set out a counterattack that forced Faku's men to flee, returning home, again, with nothing.

Gambushe was at his wit's end. His brother had tried to

convince him that he was the king the people needed, but Gambushe couldn't see it. He stayed on the battlefield with his followers, never to return home.

Alone, with no one to console him, Faku was humiliated.

What he did not know was that though his brothers laughed at his position and his ideas, his enemies, the old Bomvana chief, and the Zulu king, were aware of his potential and were slowly trying to move their captured groups away from his home in case, his true glory finally came to pass.

It did, but not in the manner that one might imagine for a Chief in wartime.

As the years went by, Faku learned that the Portuguese settlers in Africa had increased and that many of these settlers were now raiding or purchasing groups of Africans of varying ethnicities to be slaves in the growing economies of the world. This led ancient Bantu groups such as the Korana, who had so long ago shoved the Khoi toward the Cape, to work alongside the invaders in return for their own protection by raiding kingdoms and capturing slaves, which they would deliver unto the clutches of the tradesmen in the Cape. Guns and horses flowed as thick as the blood in the rivers. The British colonizers, too, were settling in rather nicely and forming their own trading ports and alliances among the people. Christianity was growing as the British ministers made their way through the kingdoms, forming alliances with chiefs and subsequently setting up posts in nearby villages. Catholicism was growing through the influence of the Portuguese, and the Dutch were seizing control over the now transformed Khoisan lands. Along with the political influences of the new company, the climate was now much hotter. Crops were dying and draining the water supply. The agricultural trade with the Europeans, although economically and financially beneficial and creating rapid growth in cities, was, in many ways, causing an equally rapid environmental collapse. The land wasn't so fertile anymore, and the cattle were starving.

All these happenings played on the new King's mind. What was he to do?

He could, like the Hintsa Gcaleka chief and the Thembu people, form a relationship with William Shaw, a British minister, and allow the clergyman to take up a post outside the border and promote Christianity in return for his people's protection. He could also rebel against them as Khoisan had tried alongside the Xhosa. Alas, those groups had both failed in their endeavors to rid themselves of colonial influences.

What if he ignored the influences, and they came for him, seeking some kind of retribution? Would he not put his people at risk?

And what of the Zulus? What of Senzagakhona's expanding kingdom? What of this proclaimed son of his, Shaka Zulu? How was he to protect his people against the Zulu raiders? What if Shaka were to feud against his true father and raid their lands too?

Faku was known for being a thoughtful chief, always thinking and always pondering the best course of action.

After careful thought, he chose to let the Zulus pass through his lands, and take what they would. After all, who of his people truly wanted to stay with him? Those who did could move closer inland, where it was safer. As for the ministers, he saw not a power among them great enough to protect him in the long run. The British, though, were an intriguing and quickly growing force, perhaps it would be best to form relationships with them.

At a crossroads, this is what the new Chief decided to do. He would stand in absolute solitude, a peacemaker among the chaos. He would make friends where he could, and leave those who called him an enemy to find resources in his land.

His choice proved to be a good one. Shaka's father, Senzakagakhona died, and Shaka became the new chief. Though there was never a feud between the relatives, Faku wasn't wrong in his assessment that blood would be spilled under Shaka's rise. Faku quickly established himself and his people as nonthreatening during the Zulu raids. This position caught Shaka's attention, and the two agreed that Faku's lands would not be disturbed so long as the routes within could be used by the Zulu Warriors on their excursions.

The minister's alliance with the Bomvana and the Thembu proved futile. When the Zulus attacked, the minister's prayers did little to save them, and the two groups were forced out of their home. Some survivors settled under the Zulu Kingdom, while the others tried to keep what was left of their histories and culture alive by seizing land from elsewhere. Faku's land would be elsewhere.

The Thembu attacked him, and he quickly repelled them, claiming his rule over the people.

More refugees settled on Mpondo lands, though most were from failed attempts at conquering Faku and his people.

Everything changed when the close allies of the Bomvana, the Tshomani, and the Baca, failed in their attempts to save their civilizations by conquering Faku's lands. Faku, not the greatest of warriors but a man who praised practice and thought above anything else, killed the Tshomani chief in battle, and his people's vision of him was forever changed.

The Bomvana chief knew that if he sided against Faku, he

may suffer the same fate. He had put much thought into war and the conquering of lands, but he had not put protections in place, and his people were in danger. The Bomvana chief formed an alliance with Faku by offering him a wife—the Bomvana chief's daughter.

Faku could have laughed at the proposal and watched his lifelong enemy fall, but he didn't.

Faku bravely turned the other cheek and wed the girl, who birthed him a son who would become a greater fighter than even Shaka Zulu.

It would be his son, Ndamase, who would go on to conquer the lands that his father would rule and later pass on to him, even though he, too, was born too late to have a rightful claim to the throne among his brothers.

If Faku taught anything to his children, it was that leadership and respect are earned through lifelong hard work. It is not a gift, but a serious and difficult job (Stapleton, 2006).

Spiritual Beliefs

The Mpondo and Thembu both fall under the Xhosa cultural and spiritual lineage.

These groups believe in the higher powers of uThixooru and his son, uQamata.

Uthixoru, the sun god, created everything on the earth, from the trees to the creatures that roamed it. In his attempt to create his people, he created the first human, and the creator of the Xhosa people, uQamata, whom he claimed as his son. uQamata went out into the world as the first human and gave rise to the others. When he died, he rose again to take a seat alongside his father. uQamata's power was unlimited and unimaginable. He was so great, that it was believed dangerous and disrespectful to call upon him and disturb his peace.

Though their gods could not and were not regularly contacted, these people communicated regularly with their ancestors, spirits of chiefs, and people who had once lived among them. Sacrifices and rituals were performed on a daily basis to appease these spirits, who could either choose to favor them or destroy them. The ancestors commonly presented themselves in the form of dreams and to chosen ones in trances.

Animals were slaughtered to feed the onlooking spirits. Honey and beer were placed in specific holy shrines for the ancestors to enjoy, and water was given plenty.

The ancestors required warmth, food, and entertainment as much as the living did. But sometimes this was not enough to appease them. The ancestors regularly sought a voice to speak through to make demands and suggestions to the people. These announcements could have dire consequences if ignored or positive ramifications if heeded and followed through. Mostly, the decision was up to the individual, or in greater cases, the chief. Depending on the situation, there might be no way to appease the ancestors without being destroyed entirely by another entity or tribe.

People who were believed to have great understanding and influence over the ancestors were sorcerers, divination seekers, healers, and herbalists. These people could influence the ancestors' whims just as easily as the ancestors could influence theirs. A sorcerer who was angry at another could influence the ancestors by providing them with good food and a good reason to inflict illness on the offending party.

When a mother among these groups gives birth, she is

required to seclude herself for ten days after giving birth so that the magic spawned by her enemies will not reach her child and destroy it. At the end of the ten days, an animal is sacrificed to appease the ancestors in the hope that they will leave the infant and mother alone permanently.

The position of diviner or sorcerer can come through either natural gifts or practice. If it's a gift, the person is merely a voice for the ancestors and isn't held responsible by the spirits for what events their messages may bring. If one practices sorcery and uses the ancestors, that person may be held accountable for their actions and those around them. They are susceptible to punishment by the spirits themselves. Practicing divination can be dark and dangerous, but it may bring glory to those who practice it well.

Herbalists and healers merely make sacrifices to the ancestors and ask for guidance in healing ailments, so they are not necessarily responsible for their messages but maybe if the ancestors so choose to use them.

Culture

The ancient culture of these people enforces the idea that men are powerful, intelligent rulers while women are intelligent and creative careers and, on most occasions, representatives of their ancestors. This belief is consistently displayed through evening entertainment such as dancing and singing. In these activities, the women will evoke the movements of their general responsibilities of caring for the children, protecting their families from evil, and conserving household resources. The men, on the other hand, evoke their memories of their battles and those of their ancestors. They display acts of hunting and leadership, and they pay tribute to the current chief by reciting poems.

The men were expected to be warriors in their own right,

strong and wealthy. When a man wanted a bride, he was to kidnap her from her home and take her as his own before proceeding with the bridal payment. In cases where the marriage was arranged, it was still expected of him to take control and ownership over his bride, that way, she would learn to respect him and see the strength in his eyes as he would learn to nurture and cherish her with everything he had.

Polygamy was common in these cultures, with men often having more than three wives. The first wife would undoubtedly have full control over the household, including the other wives. Each of the wives and their respective children would be provided with their own hut and their own resources to feed their growing family. The husband would spend equal time with each of his wives but would expect the first wife to handle disputes without his assistance. Should a wife try to sway the perception of her husband against the other wives, she would be greatly disgraced within the family.

With regard to inheritance, the firstborn son would be given ownership over his father's resources and would be expected to continue to care for his brothers and his stepmothers as well as his own growing family.

In the event that the first son is not able to take over the care of his family, the inheritance would be passed down to the next oldest son.

Until the time when the new carer was ready for marriage, his mother would take control of household duties. Once he became married, the task would be assigned to his first wife.

A man's family, which may range from about 20 to 100 individuals is considered a clan, and should the man become wealthy enough and renowned enough, he may enjoy an elite title or, if he finds difficulty in following the current chief, he may start a tribe of his own.

The chief is a man who holds massive influence over a number of people he can subsequently call his followers. One chief may rule over hundreds of thousands of clans, both rich and poor. The job of a chief is to ensure the protection, safety, and legacy of his people by going to war to obtain land and resources and by appeasing the spirits.

Folktales
Lion and the Jackal
Jackal was out hunting one day and noticed a bushbuck grazing not too far away. He looked at the bushbuck and sighed, for the buck was too big for him to catch and too heavy for him to take home to feed his family.

If only he had someone to help him catch it.

So he carried on and bumped into Lion.

"Say Lion, why don't you and I hunt together?" asked Jackal.

The Lion agreed.

"That's fine, but if we catch something small, you get to take that to your family and if we catch something big, I can take that to my family."

Jackal agreed, and the two set off.

The first animal they came across was a big eland.

"This one is mine, go to my home and call my children to take the meat."

Jackal agreed and once Lion had gone he went and called his own children to take that meat.

"How can he think I'll bring this to his family while mine are starving?" Said Jackal.

Once Lion returned home, he turned to his wife.

"How was the meat?"

"What meat?" she asked.

"Did Jackal not come and call my children to fetch the meat?" he asked.

"No," said his wife.

Lion was very angry and went to Jackal's home to confront him.

"Jackal, why did you not send for my children as I asked you to?" said Lion through the door.

But Jackal kept quiet and pretended not to be home.

The next day, Jackal got thirsty and made his way to the watering hole. Suddenly, he saw Lion's reflection in the water, so he ran and ran until he saw a little hole and flung himself in.

Lion was quick and caught Jackal's tail just in time.

"Ah, that's not my tail," said Jackal.

"Go and get a stone to smash at it with, and you'll see there is no blood."

And so Lion turned to find a stone to prove it really was Jackal's tail that he held, and when he looked back, Jackal had flung himself farther into the hole.

So Lion waited for him to come out, and Jackal lay in hiding hoping he would leave.

As the night set in and Jackal wanted to go home, he could see that the Lion was not in front of his hole waiting, but he was sure he was somewhere.

"Hello, my friend, It's me, I'm going to come out now," Jackal cried, and waited for a reply.

When none came, he scampered out of the hole and ran away.

Lion tried to catch him, but Jackal was too quick.

The next day, the Lion and Jackal had chosen to be friends again. They were hunting together when they came upon a small bushbuck.

"Here, take this thigh and go give it to my wife," said Lion, and Jackal took the thigh and gave it to his own wife.

When he returned, Lion handed him a shin. "Go and take this to your wife now," he said. Jackal took the shin to Lion's wife and upon his handing it to her, she said, "That's not mine," then Jackal slapped her with it and went back to Lion.

"Here, take this stomach to my wife," said Lion, and Jackal took the meat to his own wife.

When Lion got home, his wife was weeping and the children were scared.

"Why do you weep?" Lion asked her.

"How can you send Jackal to give me a shin and then to beat me?" she cried.

Lion was furious.

This is a tremendous tale that really explains the act of wisdom from systems of behavior and patterns (Story of the Hare, n.d.).

Chapter 13
THEMBULAND

A History

Chief Nxeko had three sons, Hlanga, Dlomo and Ndungwana. After he passed, his successor was to be Hlanga. However, after careful consideration by the council, it was decided that Hlanga did not have the qualities of a good, kindhearted, and open-minded leader. Knowing this, Dlomo, the second eldest, knew that he would have to prove himself to the council to be the leader they desired. He rallied support from the youngest brother, Ndungwana, who stood behind him as Dlomo challenged Hlanga to a stick battle for the position. Dlomo won and was proclaimed the new chief.

However, when Dlomo claimed the throne, many of the people revolted, for his position was not customary for a second-born son. These people chose to remain under Hlanga's leadership.

The late Nxeko's once united and proud nation had, in one fell swoop, been dismantled. Dlomo took those who would follow him and left, claiming lineage under a new name, the Hala.

Then there were those people who wished neither to follow Dlomo or Hlanga. These people were given to Ndungwana to rule over while pledging allegiance to victorious Hala. Ndunwana's people were titled Amandungwana.

Hlanga, despite his disposition, chose to pledge allegiance to Hala as well.

And so the Thembu nation was divided into three separate and quasi-independent kingdoms, and the people became as divided as the brothers. They worked together only out of spite and past promise.

The division got bigger over time as the Amathembu suffered falling-outs with allies and neighboring tribes, all of whom were scrambling to survive the attacks from the reigning Shaka Zulu.

Hala's wife gave birth to a son, Ukumkani, who would be the next ruler of the Amathembu.

Hala died in battle, and uKumkani was placed under a number of stresses his father had left for him to manage. In addition, the introduction of the British into Africa was plaguing uKumkani's mind and was a source of great dissatisfaction for him and his people. If the British were to attack them, his kingdom would divide further. Fearing the worst, he sought to build a relationship with the British missionaries and offered them a post.

His people were outraged, as were those in his uncles' territories. These people scrambled to find refuge under a king who would make wiser and more traditionally sound decisions. With the brothers giving support to the British, the people knew they would not find what they sought in Thembuland.

Word began to spread to the Gcaleka Hintsa, the greatest of the neighboring Xhosa nations, that Thembuland was ripe with civil unrest. The people and the chiefs were vulnerable and could be claimed under another.

The Gcaleka Hintsa attacked, taking over Amathembu little by little. They might have succeeded in claiming the entirety of the kingdom if it hadn't been for the new Cape Government having noticed the two groups' excursions along with the rest of the Mfecane fighting. The government claimed ownership over the two groups, hoping to dismantle them both.

Shaka Zulu also thought it wise to take advantage of the situation and claimed as many of the people as he could.

Then came along Madzicane of the amaBhaca, who also wanted a piece of these splintering tribes.

The survivors were afraid, alone, and bitter.

The people of Amathembuland now included a few descendants of the original tribe, hiding refugees, tortured enemies of the tribes around them, and lost clans trying to seek refuge.

uKumkani, like his father, died in battle while trying to reunite his people. His son, Bawana, wouldn't let the separation go on any longer. He decided to move the people east, out of where the Cape Government had placed them, and away from Shaka's growing army and any further threats.

If they were going to find peace as a nation and reunite as people, they needed to be secluded.

But their hopes changed to despair. They never made it to the sanctuary. Rumors of their move had spread back to the Cape Government, who sent men out to hinder and capture them.

Thembuland would never see the rejoining of its people (Mvene, 2020).

Chapter 14
XHOSALAND

A History

In Xhosaland, the position of the king was a little different from that of their neighboring tribes. A king did not rule over everyone. He, by birthright, is claimed to be the king, but his brothers, the junior chiefs, had the ability to do and say what they wanted. The king had no control over them. Each chief and king had their own group of counselors, who were the boys among their clans that had been sent on the day of the future chief's birth to work within their households. The counselors were advisors to the chiefs and would meet regularly to discuss disputes and how to better arrange the chieftains' placements within the land to avoid further conflict.

It was customary for the chief siblings to live a good distance apart from one another.

During the 1800s, as Xhosaland grew, with its chieftains spreading out and its new inhabitants—the people they subsequently conquered, they met with the now combined Khoisan groups (Maringozen, 2022).

The chieftains of Xhosaland had, along their route toward the Cape, destroyed many of the Khoisan enemies and in so doing had formed uninitiated and unexpected allies. The Khoisan gave their services to the chiefs readily and in return, were granted positions of power, wives, and wealth.

The Xhosa people had been practicing agriculture for millennia. They were not hunters, nor were they gatherers. When it came to battle, they were ferocious but inaccurate in their archery.

The Khoisan, having the experience of master huntsmen combined with master herders, were very helpful in solving this problem and trustworthy when it came to keeping the Xhosa's cherished weapons.

The Khoisan found themselves in awe of the Xhosa power and were glad to have such strong protectors among them.

Once the Dutch began to settle along the coast, the groups were glad to be on familiar terms as they battled against the Dutch for farming space. The groups would encounter one another nine times on the frontier. Eventually, the Khoi would leave, unable to fight against such skilled gunmen.

During the Xhosa chief's reign, he was tasked with securing his people against Shaka's raids while trying to expand his land and following, as well as fending off the British and the Dutch alongside his brother chieftains, he grew tired.

One day, he was invited to a meeting with the British to discuss peace between their groups. He was too tired to ask his guards to accompany him. After refusing the British terms for peace, he was shot in the head.

Devastated, his brothers would continue to fight the white colonists until their last breath (Nomedz, 2022).

CONCLUSION

And so the colonizers surrounded the people, claiming them as their own. As for the people of Africa, they would be fighting back for many years to come. Even once colonization had run its course and was long gone, the Africans are still fighting, their ancestors still calling and their hopes unhindered. Though the world may see to it that their history isn't taught with the care that the history of other continents is, they know the truth. They were there, and they remember the tales told about men who spent hours every day looking up at the stars just to count how many steps west they had taken since they set off on a hunt. They remember the stories about the women who spent hours every day singing songs and braiding hair so that they might be able to do so with rapid speed and accuracy when they were married. These people remember the moments of greatness shared among family and friends when the celebrated spoke for days on the most magical passions of their existence.

Who are we to doubt them?

History Brought Alive takes you one step further into the past and places you right there besides these glorious figures in history because once you're there, once you see it, you will never forget it.

These have all been well-researched and accounted-for theories that are widely accepted as the possibilities of a fragmented and very blotchy puzzle. There are a thousand more accepted interpretations yet to be explored.

What if the truth was that Shaka never intended to save his people from the British Colonists?

What are the chances that the Mpondo king was being swayed by his council, who were more indebted to his mother than they were to him?

And what if the Portuguese never made any of their attacks or advancements of their own accord? What if it was their embassy all along telling them what to do?

While no view is more substantial or developed than another and all have their place, History Brought Alive places the interpretations of the original people and their feelings regarding their heroes above outside voices.

Because who would know better? There is no one.

History Brought Alive has been fact-checked by dozens of helpful writers and editors alike, only using the most recent and accepted sources and arguments from well-known and respected researchers and historians.

There is nothing more poetic out there than African History. It doesn't need a snappy title or a great romance because it is already full of great deeds and legends. Here we bid farewell to some of the greatest myths and legends that ever existed

HODOO FOR BEGINNERS

CONNECT TO THE ANCIENT SPIRIT WORLD OF AFRICA & MANIFEST SUCCESS WITH SPELLS, ROOT MAGIC, CONJURING, HERBS, TRADITIONS, HISTORY & MORE

HISTORY BROUGHT ALIVE

INTRODUCTION

What is Hoodoo? Black magic, spells and conjuring, the art of healing through herbs? Ancestral rituals, talking to the spirits—folk magic?

You have to decide once you have understood how this ancient craft works.

"Hoodoo for Beginners" takes you on a journey into the mystical world of Hoodoo, rootwork, or conjuring. It is a spiritual connection that was formed between higher powers, the elements, and oppressed African-American slaves who brought over beliefs and traditions from their native Africa.

It was a secret craft created among the long-suffering people to help them form a bond of protection with the help of higher beings and their dead ancestors. Hoodoo worked through practices that taught believers about invoking the blessings and help of spirits and deities; through persuasion powers, and knowledge of healing with herbs, rituals, spell casting, talismans, and roots.

The practice earned the taboo label. Because Hoodoo invoked fear among those who did not understand the true meaning and power of the craft. It was also a threat to the slave owners and slave minders who found the power of Hoodoo growing on the great southern plantations.

This book is for the beginner feeling a strong pull toward

the traditional craft; curious to discover its heart, its lifeblood, and its rewards.

I am writing this book from personal experiences, having done more than dabble in the art of Hoodoo. Therefore, I offer you credibility. "History Brought Alive" is dedicated to creating a factual connection between the present and the past by exploring long feared folk magic, religions, and traditions.

Every book published by the company on history, mythology, and ancient crafts is backed by authenticated information to ensure the reader's eagerness to learn more about the mysticism surrounding our world is compounded with factual information. There are no hearsays or old wives' tales in this book. Everything you learn here is related to the craft and backed by credible sources. I will not feed anyone's desire to make Hoodoo dark and feared—it is so much more than that.

At the end of this book, you will become an authority on the craft as you delve deeper into the exciting world of Hoodoo step by step.

The magic of hoodoo is not fictional, nor is it a religion. It is a part of the African-American heritage; a traditional folk craft born here in North America to flourish and nurture all who respect the immense power of forming a pact between the spiritual beings of the Earth.

Hoodoo conjure was a secret craft, a form of salvation and deliverance for the entrapped slaves in the South, but 400 years since the first slaves were brought over to America, how far and deep has Hoodoo reached?

I guess it's safe to say that the practice of hoodoo is so widely popular today that it could be looking you right over the shoulder, as the craft is gaining prominence once more among the younger generation. It is no longer a secret craft, but it is still shrouded in mystique and kept veiled so others are blissfully ignorant of the great power that followers of this ancient craft wield.

"Hoodoo for Beginners" starts at the beginning. Differentiate Hoodoo from Vodou, or Voodoo, a religion originating in Western Africa and Haiti having deep roots in African culture.

Let's explore the myths and facts surrounding the craft. I will help you to understand the true nature of rootwork so you can differentiate between unrealistic theories and stories cooked up to create fear and doubt by those who do not fully understand the positive influence of Hoodoos throughout the African-American culture.

I will present you with historical facts and authenticated stories that prove the might of Hoodoo. Through each chapter, you will learn about the essential conjurer's tools for creating a bridge between the elements and spirits to harness their power and find a doorway into the spiritual world.

Gris bags, talismans, magic candles, roots, hoodoo powder, etc. and rootworkers' tools are all explained in detail.

The traditions of Hoodoo dictate that before you can call on the power of Hoodoo tools, and the spirits you must first fathom their meaning; why, how, and when each tool used in Hoodoo conjuring came to be and its significance, and the spirits responsible for granting of favors. It is only through understanding that a spiritual connection is formed between a man, the spirit world, and objects of power.

In the beginning, the heritage and roots of every African-

American, lie the secrets and power of present-day Hoodoo. Are you ready to begin your journey of discovery and empowerment?

CHAPTER 1
THE HISTORY OF HOODOO UNRAVELED

The transatlantic slave trade which created the African diaspora is greatly responsible for the birth of Hoodoo in North America. The African diaspora refers to the mass displacement of the native African people.

Hoodoo is often associated with the practice of "conjure" giving way to the popular term Hoodoo Conjure. However, Hoodoo is more than mere magic and spells.

The Antebellum era saw an influx of slaves arriving on southern plantations in North America. A majority of them worked in the fields. They were underfed, ill-treated, and lived in cramped quarters. They were no more than tools brought to serve the needs of the rich white plantation owners.

Towards the middle half of the 1800s Protestant Evangelicalism, was offered, not by choice, as a form of salvation to save the soul and many black slaves were converted to Christianity. However, unknown to the slave minders and slave owners the African people brought to work in slavery in southern plantations brought with them the knowledge of ancient religions. The worship of saints, spirits, and dead ancestors.

The religion of Vodou originated in Western Africa and is

a base on which Hoodoo was formed, although not in its entirety. The Christianity-converted slaves discovered similarities between traditional African religions and Christian beliefs. They were desperate for a source of salvation, other than what was preached at the African-American church. They needed a weapon to fight back and also a practice to seek refuge in and have their desires granted. Hoodoo was born from these needs. But Vodou/Voodoo prevalent in Haiti was banned, and so was the practice of Hoodoo. This further compounded the practice of the craft in shadowy quarters, far away from the prying eyes of the slave minders.

Therein begins the misconception that Hoodoo is to be feared, associating the practice with evil intent. The belief is that Hoodoo is all about the desecration of graves, zombies, and the creation of spells and hexes to cause harm. The stigma attached to Hoodoo has prevented those practicing the craft from openly declaring the true intent of this traditional North American practice which is a marvelous synthesis of religions, native knowledge, and traditional beliefs prevalent among the diverse ethnicities on the North American continent.

Hoodoo is not to be confused with Voodoo—or Vodou—although all practices have emerged from African culture. Instead, Hoodoo has its roots in Christianity. With more similarities to Christianity that is let on.

Hoodoo was branded as superstition. The label is awarded to any practice for which the masses do not have a proper understanding. In other words, a practice that is not a mainstream belief.

Let's not forget that in ancient Rome, Christianity was banned similarly. Treated like a cult following, and those who practiced Christianity did so in secret, holding mass in hidden quarters fearing the punishment that followed anyone who was found out to be a believer of Christ.

The practice of Hoodoo Conjure did not soar to the heights of popularity that Christianity did; the practice remains in the shadows, although modern followers no longer hide their beliefs.

To understand the roots of Hoodoo in America, we must first look at its beginnings which were amongst the African slaves who followed the teachings, rituals, and customs of the West African religion of Voodoo.

In this chapter, we will look at the evolution of hoodoos on the North American Continent. How a practice shrouded in superstition bearing a reputation of being evil, survived over the centuries to become a folk religion in the US. Is it possible this traditional craft has gained its strength through time by integrating its beliefs through culture?

It's safe to establish that Hoodoo survived mainly due to its acceptance as a sort of folk religion. Which relies on beliefs, rituals, and practices being passed on from one generation to the next as a traditional cultural heritage.

Still, Hoodoo is not a religion, it is a heritage; therefore, when you seek to know more about Hoodoo you are delving deeper into the legacy, traditions, practices, and culture of the African—American slaves and their descendants.

How it All Started, Vodou and Hoodoo? The Beginnings

The African diaspora is mainly responsible for the birth of Hoodoo conjure or rootwork in North America. In case you have not heard of the term, let me explain.

The African diaspora refers to the mass displacement of

the native African people.

Millions fell prey to the slave trade which flourished between 1500 to 1800. People from Central and Western Africa were forcefully taken to feed the Transatlantic Slave Trade, ending up across the American continent; with the Caribbean acting as a hub from where many were transhipped to the Americas.

The first slaves to enter North America came to Virginia in 1619. And so the South became the most prominent North American region for slavery, and subsequently, the birthplace of Hoodoo.

Hoodoo became both a protector and weapon for fighting against the injustices suffered by the African-American people. Freed slaves and those still in bondage relied on Hoodoo as a form of spiritual healing. It was a link to their African heritage and also a weapon to rebel against their oppressors.

The practice of "conjure" came with the African slaves, but before we move on to Hoodoo Conjour it is important to understand the traditions, beliefs, and customs of connecting religions that served as a base for the formation of Hoodoo.

How Much Do You Know About Vodou?

I would describe Vodou as the seed from which Hoodoo came into existence.

Vodou is an ancient belief; a religion that originated in the Western African nations of South Benin, Nigeria, and Togo—the region was called the Kingdom of Dahomey up until the 1970s, now called Benin.

Another name for Dahomey is Fon, it is also the name of the language used by the Dahomey people who are known as

Fon nu.

Fon is similar to Ewe, a language spoken in South Togo, South Benin, and Ghana, it is known as the common language among the Kwa people who come from the Niger-Congo region.

Vodou is the Fon name for 'spirit' or 'god' and is also spelled as Vodou or Vodon. It is a singular religion practicing the worship of one almighty deity. Hence, Vodou is based on monotheism. Much like Christianity.

Mawu-Lisa the pantheon of all deities also called Mahou-Lisa, or Mahu-Lisa refers to the female deity Mahu/Mawu and Lisa her husband— the creators.

In Dahomey mythology, the pair are one—described as the sun and the moon. Vodou is the worship of one primary deity (monotheism). Or in this case the creators of heaven and earth.

The female entity Mawu is the moon. She symbolizes night; together with fertility, motherhood, joy, gentleness, forgiveness, and rest. These are, as you will notice, the epitome of the female gender.

Lisa is the sun; the male entity. He is associated with the day; war, strength, toughness, power, and steadfastness. A paragon for the stronger sex.

In Haitian Vodou, this supreme entity is known as Gran Met or Bondye/Bonye. An all-powerful God who is also transcendent.

The New-World Afro-diasporic vein of Vodou practiced in Haiti is a combination of European, African, and traditional Taino religious beliefs. The Taino are an indigenous race of people from the Caribbean. Most sources link Vodou's beginnings to Haiti. Where the craft evolved and became stronger among the slaves working in the direst of conditions on the vast plantations there.

Vodou in Haiti

Haitian Vodou emerged around the 16th century; it began as an amalgamation of traditional West African beliefs and Christianity which was fast spreading through colonization. Therefore, Bondye quite often shares a link with the God of Christianity, who is identified as the beginning and the end. The all-powerful in whose hands lie the fate of men.

However, Vodou is not as straightforward as explained thus far.

Contradicting the theory of Vodou being a monotheistic religion there is a belief in spirits. Deity worship in African culture is categorized as the worship of primary, secondary, and tertiary gods. Therefore, the Lwa, pronounced as Iwah, exists as part of Vodou's polytheistic belief in secondary gods.

The lwa are called by many names, loa, loi, mystères, saints, anges (angels), Les Invisibles. In Vodou, there are thousands of lwa who act as intermediates to Mawa-Lisa or Bondye on behalf of men. Again there is a similarity to Christianity where the intercession of saints and angels on behalf of man is a part of the belief.

Spirit Possession

An important element in Vodou is possession. Possession allows the lwa, to bond with a man.

Vodouism believes in the possession of a man's spirit/soul; possession is a method of unification between man and God.

Devotees go on to describe their experience of being possessed as "being ridden like horses by the lwa" they allow the lwa to take control of the reins. It is described as giving in to the desire of being owned by the spirits during the period of possession. This is seen as a means of fulfilling the desires of both the spirit and man. The possession by a spirit is often seen as a process of healing, divine intervention, and answers to one's problems.

The practice of Vodou is overseen by priestesses, known as the mambo or manbo (the latter is a derivation of the Fon word for 'mother of magic'—nanbo). The male equivalent is an oungan.

In both the Western African and Haitian versions of Hodou, it is the priestess who oversees the rituals, prays for healing, and intercedes as a bridge between the gods, and the spirits, on behalf of the faithful. Initiation into the priesthood requires a series of trials to be performed. Increasing the priest's konesan, (their sacred knowledge) is the ultimate goal of each trial.

Vodou is a structured religion; a complex web of intricately woven traditions, rituals, and beliefs. It is important to understand these basics for you to get a grasp of where Hoodoo begins.

One final point I wish to make before moving on is the clarification of the term Voodoo. The more popular and glamorized name was given to the folk religion predominantly by Hollywood.

Voodoo a Carefully Constructed Image of Black Magic, Vengeance, and Death

The name Voodoo invokes images of black magic rituals, dolls stuck with pins, graveyards, and zombies for many. Fear and dread are associated with the name which is a carefully marketed brand to keep the image of evil associated with the craft.

In English, Creole, and French, the correct term for the religion is Vodou, derived from the fon name of Vodoun. The derogatory term in which the name Voodoo is used emerged around the 1920s after the 1915 occupation of Haiti by the US.

Voodoo grew in popularity as people lapped up the bacchanalias-type rituals, witchcraft, and evil sorcery associated with Voodoo presented as an uncivilized religious practice on the island. The image was given prominence through the movies and carefully spun stories; the American public lapped it all up with eager disgust.

Therefore, the name Voodoo to this day is associated with evil black magic with the intent of harm; the association of the ancient religion with Christianity is lost in the perverted image of Vodou through Voodoo.

Many believe the US occupation of Haiti at the time was responsible for this twisted portrayal of Vodou as a means to justify the actions of the US government.

Here's what Professor of Arficology Patrick Bellegarde-Smith, from the University of Wisconsin-Milwaukee had to say.

"The word 'voodoo' comes out of Hollywood in the 1920s, '30s, '40s as the United States was occupying Haiti, and it served to justify the occupation to a large extent in the eyes of Americans," (VodouOrVoodoo, n.d.)

CHAPTER 2
THE BIRTH OF HOODOO

Hoodoo, Conjure, or Rootworking all refer to the same ancestral practice or craft born in North America. Hoodoo evolved from a need, a need for the protection and salvation of the African slave suffering under dire conditions in a foreign land.

The people of Africa, stolen from their homeland brought with them the knowledge of an ancient folk religion—Vodou. Which was highly prevalent in Haiti, a hub for the dispersion of slaves to the North American continent.

Healing, divine intervention, and spiritual protection is the promise of Hoodoo, and not the corrupted version viewed in the US of black magic, hedonism, casting hexes, and sorcery used for evil purposes against society.

Vodou, an ancient religion, was already being viewed as a primitive form of evil magic practiced in Africa. It was convenient for slave owners to categorize the practices of the enslaved people as evil and primitive as a means to justify the western imperialistic tactics adopted by slave traders; this perception was further endorsed by Christian missionaries intent on "saving the souls" of the primitive people practicing black magic.

The areas of North Carolina and Georgia were soon populated by African slaves brought in from the Congo and

Angola regions. With them, they brought knowledge of ancient Western African folk religions. These people suffered many atrocities. They were tortured, starved, and overworked.

Therefore a great need, a huge hunger, for justice prevailed among the enslaved people of Africa, and it is from this enormous need that Hoodoo was born. Born out of the souls of dead slaves whose spirits empowered the first conjurers to discover the power and a weapon to fight back spiritually through Hoodoo.

Spirit worship dominated the African traditional religions; spirits of the dead ancestors, spirits of the land, and deities worshiped on the African continent were venerated. However, all that was going to change as the African slaves were influenced by the teachings and supernatural beliefs of the new religions and ethnicities they became exposed to.

The Influence of Christianity on Hoodoo

The Black Code or Code Noir governing slavery within the French colonies, declared, that slaves be baptized into the Christian religion.

The enslaved people were offered salvation in the form of forced baptism into Christianity. In doing so the missionaries unwittingly revealed to the African people that Christianity was quite similar to the deeply spiritual aspects awarded to Vodou, and other traditional religions born on the African continent.

The worship of one divine God, Mawu-Lisa, and the intervention of the lwa spirits, as is the belief of the Fon nu people of Dahomey had strong similarities to the supernatural characteristics of Christianity which too was centered on spirits and saints, Jesus Christ and a supreme God. Let me remind you once more about the similarity of Christianity centered on the Holy Trinity the Father, Son, and Holy Spirit. And of Voudon on the creators, the Sun and Moon (Mawu-Lisa).

The connection between the one true God of Christians, and Bondye/Grand Met, the supreme creator worshiped in Haitian Vodou, and the belief in spirits and saints led to the manifestation of a divine practice the enslaved people found comfort and safety.

It was a unique underground practice born among the African-American community using the fragments of their traditional ancestral religions from Africa, and the connection found in the teachings of European religions such as Christianity, as well as the native religious practices, and knowledge of herbalism from the indigenous people in the new land they were enslaved in, the Native American Indians.

As a practice shrouded in the European religion of Christianity, the enslaved people were thus able to follow their banned craft of hope and protection inside Black-American Christian churches and at the same time satisfy their capturers' needs to offer them salvation through Christianity. To this day, there are many Christian prayers used in the performance of Hoodoo rituals.

A fine example is how possession, a key component of Vodou and Hoodoo, was hidden in the open as part of the black American church culture.

The 'Christian' slaves practiced what was called "Catching the Holy Ghost." The term in Christianity's belief revolves around faith in saints and giving up one's spirit to the Holy Ghost to fulfill a desire or need which is very much how possession in Hoodoo works. And so, in this guise, the slaves were practicing possession in Hoodoo where spirits were invoked to take possession.

There are many similarities between Hoodoo and Christianity which the black slaves used to their advantage, mostly to avoid punishment and death which was the fate dealt out to anyone caught practicing the taboo religion of Voodoo.

Hoodoo saints and spirits were openly worshiped under the guise of Catholic saints; the supernatural entities were venerated while prayers and psalms similar to Christianity were used for healings and rituals.

African slaves who adopted the European religion of Christianity did not find it a necessity to abandon their traditional religious beliefs. Instead, they found a way to easily merge the two to form a new practice—Hoodoo.

Native American Influences in Hoodoo

Native Americans were among the first slaves in Louisiana, which was the homeland of the indigenous people of North America and the place where Hoodoo evolved.

The many Native American tribes that were held in bondage were soon joined by the African slaves brought over during the Transatlantic Slave Trade. As is to be expected, the two groups bonded, planning escape routes and sharing their traditional beliefs and knowledge of roots, herbs, and spirits that resided in the land, the animals, the rain, water, trees, and plants.

And so Hoodoo was born as a marvelous amalgamation of African Traditional Religions, Native American beliefs and practices, folk magic, spirits of nature, the divine intervention of saints, supernatural powers, and Christianity. The dominant characteristics of Hoodoo, however, come from

African Traditional Religions. Although Hoodoo is more a native North American practice while Vodou is traditional African folk religion.

The New American Folk Religions—Hoodoo

The practice was a combination of spirits from Haitian Vodou, the lwas and mystères, the archangels and saints from Catholicism, the spirits of the Native Americans, spirits of the ancestors, and of course zombies which you will learn more of when we explore the pantheon of Hoodoo.

It was a hearty mix of new spirits and those from traditional African beliefs. The supernatural was coupled with symbols, sacred rituals, dances, prayer, and songs also borrowed as an influence from other religious practices.

Therefore, it is largely believed that European customs and beliefs too had a great influence on the creation of Hoodoo.

Many evolutions took place among the African slaves exposed to the diverse religious and supernatural customs of the new land.

- Traditional African religious practices and rites seen as pagan rituals were largely abandoned.
- African words used in Hoodoo, compared to Vodou, became less and were replaced by English words. For example, in Vodou, a male priest is houngan, and a priestess mambo from the Fon language. But in Hoodoo you get the rootworker, the goopher doctor, the cunning man, the high man, and other typical English terms. They were best known as Gullah among the African slaves.
- African, Native American, and Christian supernatural customs were adopted to create magico-religious practices.

- The emergence of new beliefs, rituals, and customs takes into account elements from European religious beliefs, African traditional religions, and Native American myths and practices.

Hoodoo was a hybrid practice, a cross between cultures, a synthesis of beliefs with one purpose—improving and protecting the lives of enslaved black people, giving them hope and a better chance at achieving their desires.

Therefore, Hoodoo is a practice embedded with rituals for healing the body, mind, and soul, seeking divine intervention for good luck and well-being, and for the protection of the African-American community.

It is magico-religious; referring to a craft using magical practices to seek supernatural intervention for the granting of favors and obtaining specific needs.

Therefore, Hoodoo became the additional support when religion alone did not deliver and ease the suffering of the enslaved African-American community.

The Problem Rituals and Beliefs of the Black Slaves—Hoodoo

Authorities on Hoodoo emerged, and the practice spread widely, by the 19th century, among the enslaved African-American population.

Followers of the craft or Hoodooists were called many names; conjure women and men, root doctors, Hoodoo doctors, soothsayers, spirit workers, two heads, and so on and so forth. These authorities on Hoodoo were credited with having special knowledge of the spirit world, the sacred arts, roots, herbs, rituals, and granting blessings.

In Virginia and Maryland the term cunning doctors, high women/men was common as the more popular English or white man terms used for those who practiced "good magic".

There never were priests or priestesses, as there are in Vodou, but then Hoodoo is not a religion. It is a practice open to anyone as curious and devoted as you are to learn more about the divine powers that govern the power of Hoodoo.

Hoodoo grew in popularity as a secret practice among the enslaved black plantation workers at the height of slavery, and Hoodoo doctors, conjurers, or spirit workers with supernatural powers became popular; they were seen as a form of salvation and powerful rebellion against the slave masters.

These teachers or practitioners of Hoodoo were sought out by African-American society for many needs. For healing various types of physical ailments, offering protective spells against threatening forces such as the slave breakers, making people fall in love, improving one's fortune or riches, and even retrieving objects that were lost. They were the local folk doctors of sorts who performed "good magic" aiding the everyday needs of the black community.

However, there is good and bad to all magic, and Hoodoo Conjure is no exception. The exploited and vulnerable state of the oppressed black slaves led to the manifestation of a darker version of Hoodoo being practiced.

Let's not forget though that Hoodoo's purpose was the protection of the black slaves from harm, violence, and suffering. The belief that a higher power could be called on was needed for the healing of mind and body. Therefore, Hoodoo magic was used at times for revenge, retaliation, and also as a form of retaliation on behalf of the helpless.

Aggressive and threatening forms of magic, as well as cursing, are seen as heathen practices which belong to uncultured peoples and are therefore feared, and categorized as a taboo form of black magic. But, let me remind you that aggression and cursing are both present in other religions.

Christianity for example; one instance is where Noah saved the Israelis from bondage in Egypt after several aggressive acts against the Pharaoh and his people. The land was cursed several times with the death of the firstborns in all Egyptian homes being the final trial. Again, here is a fine example of spirituality, or faith, being used as a tool for the "greater good".

Hoodoo was always an underground practice, which at times hid in plain sight under Christian rituals. The stigma that was awarded to Vodou better known as Voodoo in its carefully constructed image of evil black magic was banned in North America.

Practicing conjure and Voodoo were seen as venues for instigating rebellion amongst the slaves. The negative impact of the craft on the slave trade was taken quite seriously with legal action often being implemented to squash any possibility of an uprising.

A good example is when around the 19th century the governors of Louisiana banned the import of slaves from Santo Domingo and Martinique on the premise that they possessed a penchant for the practice of Vodou or Voodoo.

Segregating the Practise of Hoodoo

Let's break down the practice of Hoodoo.

Hoodoo has its roots in African Traditional Religions which focus on ancestral devotion, seeking spiritual protection, and herbal healing. The root work and herbal healing knowledge, as well as the power of spirits from nature, were learned from the Native Indians. While the supernatural aspect of Christianity greatly influenced and helped shroud the practice of the slave minders.

Root and Rootworking

This does not refer to working with roots alone as one would envision from the name.

Roots in the literal context will refer to the entire plant and not just the root. It will include all parts of the plant including the seed, stem, and petals—think of 'root' as an umbrella term.

Rootwork in its entirety is the use of natural objects from nature similar to herbalism, as well as organic substances (including animals) for performing rituals, and spells to make events happen in relation to healings or even causing harm.

Hands—or gris bags—and Goopher dust, which is very much a part of traditional African magic, were for example made by root doctors to be used as talismans of protection and even for vengeance. The dust was collected from graveyards and the practice is considered one of the most important links Hoodoo retains with its African heritage.

Native American contributions toward the healing power a Hoodooist or root doctor possessed were wide. There was at least one Gullah (rootworker) on every plantation, and slaves put their trust in this healer while eyeing the white physicians with distrust.

The use of roots for both healing and casting spells was used, hence the name two heads were often given to rootworkers. The Ginseng root, a symbol of male fertility, was favored amongst the root doctors for both its curative powers, and as a vessel for supernatural influences. The "walking man" is often the reference given to a charmed ginseng root.

Divination or supernatural predictions too were achieved

through rootwork. For example; if a root doctor was asked to put a root on a person, it would involve a supernatural element. In this ritual, goofer dust was turned into a powerful concoction of dried lizard or snake powder mixed with dirt from a graveyard. This was to be rubbed on the person seeking the favor, to cause harm to another, to prevent it from befalling the believer, or even make someone fall in love.

A rootworker had many skills; mojo bags were another method of offering supernatural protection/help for a specific purpose. Often a dime would be tied around the ankle or a small sack containing both plant and animal parts would be worn around the neck.

Hoodoo Conjuring
Conjur or conjuring—the casting of spells, refers to the bridge created between the spirits of dead people, angels, and saints as well as other divine beings from the spirit world.

Ancestors and even Jesus Christ as well as supernatural elements from Christianity will be included in Hoodoo Conjur. Factors that create that strong bond between Hoodoo and other traditional religions.

Although connected deeply to religion, "magic" has also garnered a lot of negative publicity throughout the ages. The persecution of witches throughout European history is testament enough to the huge element of fear created by black magic. Going back to the example of Moses; he was able to match the magic of the sorcerers in Pharaoh's court by turning water to blood, and his staff into a snake.

Practitioners and opponents of Hoodoo magic have over the ages acquired, recreated, and even criticized the craft. Although viewed as a vile opponent to orthodox religious beliefs, it is in fact a reflection of the essence on which most religions are based.

Powerful slaves who were known as conjure men/women gained the respect of their fellow slaves. But they were also sought out by the white slave owners who often visited them for their very accurate soothsaying powers. These conjure men wielded a sense of dark power and were often left alone by slave owners and slave minders who feared and believed the many stories of supernatural retaliation that were spreading in the south.

Modern Young African-American Christians Find a Connection With Hoodoo

Hoodoo which began to spread rapidly in the 1800s is an accepted and widespread practice in our modern times. Although the stigma of the practice being bad still sticks among the ignorant.

Scholars have researched the history of Hoodoo making a wealth of information available to the curious, which is no longer limited to just the African-American community.

Christian youth are trying to understand and connect with their African heritage. Most of that heritage happens to be linked to Hoodoo which to their surprise has deep links to Christianity making it easier for them to continue their Christian beliefs while delving deeper into their ancestral religions.

These youngsters are deciding for themselves, trying to dispel the myths put in place during the 18–19th centuries, by white supremacy, and the Christian churches, that Hoodoo and most traditional African religions are pagan rituals, dark and evil practices with an intent to harm.

They are exploring practices centered on traditional African cosmology, and at the same time learning about herbal healing powers, the power found within ancestral objects and communicating with spirits. Therefore, these youngsters are able to determine for themselves how the power of Hoodoo is used and its true context when it comes to determining its good and bad traits.

The Evolution of Hoodooism Over Time

The Antebellum era or you may better know it as the 'Great Plantation Period' is when Hoodoo really grew in strength. This was the time from around the mid-1800s to the beginning of the American Civil War which commenced in 1861.

The conjure men that evolved during this period offered the slaves protection from the cruel actions of the slave minders. These rootworkers offered protection together with other healing services, as well as supernatural services such as soothsaying.

As such their fame grew and so did their power with the strongest conjure men being left alone to go about their business as even the white slave minders feared their reputation.

Some of the famous conjure women and men you should read up on include Dr. Buzzard, Aunt "Zippy" Tule, Aunt Caroline Dye, and Dr. Jim Jordan; they are not from the Antebellum era, instead, these powerful conjurers used their power and fame to both help the public and grow rich. For example, Jim Jordan was able to amass considerable wealth and owned numerous companies by the time he died in 1962.

The most loved was probably Aunt Caroline Dye who went on to become one of the most prominent conjure women in and around Newport, Arkansas; her soothsaying powers were renowned. Aunt Caroline Dye passed away in 1918 and is said to have used her powers for only good.

The Three Elements of Hoodoo

You may have asked yourself the question, "is Hoodoo real?" several times before deciding to pick up this book.

To everyone who has experienced the craft, yes it is.

However, you must come to that discovery on your own once you have journeyed through your learning process. I will go on to explain the three elements on which the craft of Hoodoo works, and gains the faith of its followers.

A religion becomes real through faith. You pray to Gods and saints because you believe they exist and are listening to you.

How your prayers are answered depends on the extent of your belief, and how deep and steadfast your faith is coupled with how much of the supernatural element you believe in without doubt or question.

Hoodoo, although not a religion, works along the same lines—it is real and based on trust and the virtue of those practicing the craft. It continues to exist and interact with believers, therefore it is real.

A craft that was formed as an amalgamation of several religions but not categorized as a religion is hard to fully comprehend. Yet Hoodoo has withstood the test of time not letting down believers.

To Understand How Hoodoo Made it Into the 21st Century Let's Look at Its Basic Elements

The enslaved people of Africa, many by then born into slavery in America and not Africa, toward the latter parts of the 1800s, started to rely on Hoodoo doctors for healing, physically and mentally.

The natural herbs and roots used by rootworkers as curative concoctions do in fact have strong connections to herbal medicinal remedies and offer the same curative promises the medicine prescribed by a physician does. Let's not forget that Hoodoo is also magico-religious, stepping in when religion fails to deliver.

The use of supernatural powers and conjuring offers the desired result where root doctors create talismans from roots and other objects to grant the seekers what they desire. In the past, these talismans, hands, and gris bags were quite often worn for protection against the slave breakers.

It was a case of fixing the mind to believe in the magic in order for it to work, although there are accounts registered by skeptics who witnessed the true power of an enchanted talisman.

Hoodoo Works and Manifests Its Powers on the Following Three Elements.

1. *The Use of Natural Organic Remedies for Healing*

Herbalism and other organic substances, as I mentioned before, are similar to those used by the Native Americans who shared their vast knowledge of the curative powers of herbs, roots, and plants.

2. *The Placebo Effect Functions on Faith and Perception.*

The belief in something that would otherwise be incomprehensible. Spells, concoctions, and magical talismans promise to give the seeker what they desire, mostly catering to a desire that would otherwise be hard to manifest on their own.

Belief makes the crafts' power real. Placebos can be inert procedures or objects which are used in Hoodoo rituals.

The mind plays a huge role in the success of Hoodoo magic. Therefore, the placebo effect works in the context of mind over matter—the power of suggestion.

People seeking the help of rootworkers value their power, place faith in their ability to deliver their desires, and are eager to follow instructions that lead to favorable results.

The belief in the conjure man/woman's power to heal is similar to the belief you place in contemporary doctors and the medicine they prescribe.

You believe the pills you ingest are going to make you well. In most instances, this psychological influence does make you feel better. Let's not forget the actual curative effect of the components in the medicine that work to heal. But believing in medicine makes you accept its curative abilities which do contribute to the healing process. This phenomenon is further compounded through studies proving its effects.

Hoodoo works in the same way, the believer's faith in the root doctor causes them to accept the spiritual healing promised, by opening their minds and placing trust in the supernatural which in part contributes to the remedy working.

3. The Nocebo Effect, the Negative Phenomenon

Now here's the flip side of the placebo effect, the negative aspect of believing in a favorable outcome. Here again, mind over matter works negatively to cause harm.

A nocebo effect is the harboring of negative thoughts that can cause harm to a person physically and mentally. Those thoughts could be self-achieved or planted in your mind through the power of suggestion.

Think about it, if a relatively healthy person is suddenly

diagnosed with cancer, they are suddenly going to be burdened with the negative effects of the illness. Although they lived normal healthy lives before the diagnosis the implication of suffering from the terminal illness will cause rapid degeneration of their physical being. Because the mind has suddenly been told the body is unwell.

To prove the effects of the nocebo phenomenon, a study was conducted where some patients undergoing a test were told it would be painful while the rest were told it was a simple painless exercise.

The results proved the power of suggestion worked with the groups. The batch, already informed of the probability of pain, found the test 'painful' while the other half had no experience of discomfort (Pfingsten et al., 2001).

The power of suggestion when wielded by a clever Hoodooist can be quite influencing and damaging when used to cause mischief or to gain vengeance.

For example, a person being told that they are under a curse that will cause their death, will upon accepting the suggestion, let the thought corrupt their mental being which in turn will influence their physical being until death does become a reality. That is the power of suggestion and the third element on which Hoodoo works.

Despite Hoodoo having the power to cause harm, it is still a practice created to protect and nurture the well-being of the African-American community, although today Hoodoo offers protection to a wider spectrum of believers regardless of race.

It is still predominantly a healing practice much like that of a physician. The rationale and ingredients used for cures may be different but the goals remain the same. That is the true essence of Hoodoo and one you must grasp fully before you move on to the next chapter, "Getting Started With Hoodoo".

There you can learn more about the myths and legends surrounding the craft as well as the material used to create the charms, and other devices used as vessels for the supernatural to wield their power.

CHAPTER 3
GETTING STARTED WITH HOODOO

The authentication of Hoodoo in the 21st century has been questioned many times. In the previous chapter, you read about the interest young African-American Christians were showing in their heritage and in particular the craft of Hoodoo.

These people are desperately seeking sources to authenticate the factors that define this traditional North American folk magic.

They are navigating through the weeds of carefully sown seeds of doubt that portray Hoodoo as a taboo craft and a hoax, and a form of black magic that is best left alone.

That is a tough image to change.

Still, Hoodoo has existed and has even been glamorized over the years, its true nature and power exalted by the many believers who today go beyond the Black-American society. But because of the commercialized image of Hoodoo, not everyone who claims to be a Hoodooist is a true one.

Only the people of African heritage are able to perform Hoodoo, due to their ability to call on the spirits of their oppressed ancestors the slaves whose deaths helped manifest the practice.

Getting started with Hoodoo requires you to learn the

basics. You already explored its history and you know the craft is unique to the diverse North American culture.

Since Hoodoo is not a religion but a practice, a novice believer is able to get started with the craft in an almost "do it yourself" pattern where you start off by forming a connection with your African heritage—the spirits of your ancestors. You must also get familiar with how Hoodoo works. The rules, the material used, and the beliefs. Keep in mind that Hoodoo is not a craft that you can practice on the spur of the moment. You cannot cast a spell or tie root and expect it to work if you have not been following the general norms of the craft on a daily basis. Daily cleansing rituals and giving thanks to ancestors must be followed on a regular basis before you can ask the spirits and saints for help.

It is true Hoodoo is greatly commercialized, a concept that started with the urbanization of African-American communities around the 1920s and 1930s. This shift in status led to Hoodoo becoming a glitzy money-earning commodity. Authentic root workers were replaced by celebrity conjurers.

Previously handmade charms, gris bags, and mojo bags started to disappear, and in their place, ready-made charms, potions, powders, and talismans to serve every need started to appear in specialized shops that sold everything from love potions to hexes.

Therefore, to get started with Hoodoo, the true Hoodoo, the folk practice created as an amalgamation of the different ethnicities that formed a bond of suffering during the height of the North American slave trade, you must learn about the real tools and methods used by the conjure men and women born into slavehood on the great Southern plantations.

In this chapter you will learn about the workings of

Hoodoo; learn about crossroads, spiritual baths, and working tricks with the aid of roots, crystals, and herbs. Hoodoo is not a craft that you can pick up on the spur of the moment, you cannot make a mojo bag from instructions online and expect it to work. You must know the significance of each ingredient put in that pouch, and how they interact with each other to create more power. You must build up your faith and convince the spirits, offer daily prayers to the ancestors, and confirm your intentions as a true believer; it is only then that you can step into the realm of Hoodoo conjure and expect the magic to work.

How Does Hoodoo Work? Spirits, Places, and Tools

Most newcomers to Hoodoo start off with a simple conjure, a ritual to manifest a blessing or initiate a simple change in their situation.

Hoodoo is popular not simply because it becomes a powerful and accessible tool for all believers, but for the benefits of practicing conjure, which you too can easily learn and master through daily rituals, faith and practice.

Hoodoo is often sought out for the following benefits.

- Protection—herbs, and roots are used to create mojo bags that can be worn for protection. Popular ingredients used to create protection mojo bags are basil and morning glory. The Angelica root too is a popular root for protection. It can be added to a mojo bag and hung around your neck or in a room to which you seek to offer protection. Make sure the mojo/Gris bag is not visible to anyone. If seen or touched by anyone other than the beneficiary of the bag, the charm will lose its power.
- Manifestation—Hoodoo is also popular for its power of

manifestation. You can ask the spirits to grant your desires by manifesting them. Placing your intentions in an offering at a crossroads or inside a mojo bag will help you to reach your desires through the intercession of the spirits in the roots you use.

- Wealth and good luck—are other attractions of Hoodoo. You can practice creating mojo bags to attract luck with a combination of the following ingredients. John the Conqueror root, luck hand root, a rabbit's foot, and fast luck oil. Fast Luck Oil is very popular for attracting good fortune at gambling games, rubbing some oil on your lottery tickets, and even on Bingo cards. Sudden and fast windfalls are guaranteed when believers use the oil which is often a combination of olive oil and botanicals such as juniper, cinnamon, rose, fenugreek, etc.

Before Hoodoo was 'glamorized', rootworkers looked for their tools in nature.

Some examples of popular tools used include the John the Conqueror root, chewing John roots, black cat bones, five-finger grass, and devil's shoestring.

These tools of Hoodoo were blessed by the supernatural following rituals performed by the rootworkers. They were then handed over to the believers as talismans and mojo charms for obtaining desired goals.

Hoodoo beliefs too change from region to region, the reason being that in each part of the continent, the influences that shaped Hoodoo were different. The south, for example, home to slaves brought in from Angola and Congo, influenced Hoodoo practices with Western African beliefs.

The unique and slight differences in how a family practiced

Hoodoo were passed down from generation to generation until the changes became a distinctive characteristic of a family's Hoodoo practice.

A Hoodoo conjurer uses various materials to manifest a spell. Animal parts, including bones, herbs, and other botanicals, and minerals such as salts and oils. Bodily fluids such as semen, menstrual blood, and urine are the most common when a spell is being performed for personal gain, distancing, or revenge.

The commonest reasons believers visit a rootworker/conjurer to obtain favors are centered on love, luck, money, revenge, divination, health, employment, and intimate relationship problems.

Modern-Day Hoodooism

A visit to the nearest spiritual shop will reveal to you a wonderful world of ready-made Hoodoo tools. Plus additional items such as color-coded candles with pre-cast spells, enchanted oils, and even sprays. They are far from the natural material the traditional conjurer picked up in the wild. Instead, these are synthetic substances made in factories supplying the modern Hoodoo industry. Likewise, there are people who practice the craft as a commercial commodity, most of these people are false Hoodooists (although some genuine Hoodooist will at times go on to benefit from their power). Hence, it is important to find a verified Hoodooist to further your interest in the craft.

None of those tools whether authentic or commercially bought will work if you cannot make a connection with the spirits of your ancestors, and to do so you must understand the rules of Hoodoo conjure.

While traditional Hoodooist offered believers their

services through working tools gathered from scavenging the woods and fields, the modern believer can simply visit the nearest spiritual shop to pick up their supplies. The shops in turn receive stocks from manufacturers who supply them with their zoological and botanical charms. For either to work you must be a believer, make that important connection with your heritage and practice the craft within the parameters of balance.

The Rules and Parameters of Hoodoo Conjure

Conjures' primary goal is to initiate change or to manifest a change in the believer's situation. Sometimes a change is done through the manipulation of a circumstance.

Divination or reading-on a believer will help the root worker to define the problem. If the person seeking help is having problems the root worker can through divination find the source. Sometimes it turns out to be a hex put there by someone else, sometimes it could be a block of energy or closed doors at the crossroads of life.

Since Hoodoo is an amalgamation of the Christian religion, it is common practice to use Psalms from the Bible during a conjuring ritual. Therefore, it is not uncommon for rootworkers to be known as Catholics. This is common in predominantly Catholic areas such as South Carolina and New Orleans where rootworkers will even attend Sunday mass.

A fine example of the integration of Catholicism into Hoodoo conjure is the veneration of Catholic saints, the use of Catholic symbols during rituals, and the recital of psalms and prayers.

Many Hoodoo conjurers even call the Bible their book of spells. The Bible is often taken to the crossroads as a weapon of protection against the evil spirits that resided. Also, rootworkers are able to decipher the psalms to use as spells to offer cures for marital problems, simple headaches, and good luck for safe travel.

Often a rootworker working on a ritual to remove a hex put on a person will quote verses from the Bible to drive out the evil influence.

Christian similarities extend to the saints of Hoodoo too with many from the Christian religion being invoked through roots. Saint Expedite was a Roman soldier who was executed for his conversion to Christianity, and in Hoodoo he is venerated as a saint to grant speedy solutions to problems that cannot wait or to end any type of delay that may be causing problems for the believer. Expedite is also the saint for overcoming procrastination and he is portrayed stamping down on a crow because the caw-caw of a crow is supposed to symbolize the phrase tomorrow-tomorrow. These are only a few examples of the similarities Hoodoo shares with Christianity.

The Importance of Night and Day in Hoodoo

When practicing Hoodoo you will learn that the realms of night and day co-exist, as mirrors of each other—alternate realities.

Therefore the spirits have the power to influence how your life turns out through manifestation. An important aspect of Hoodoo's spiritualism is balance. You must learn to maintain a balance between both worlds. And when both realities become the same you can expect that change you desire.

You must also learn about the spirits in roots and the fundamentals that govern both the world of the living and the world of the dead. You must get a grasp of the positive and negative powers that a Hoodooist can wield. Remember that maintaining a balance between the elements of good and bad is important to work real magic through Hoodoo and enjoy its benefits.

The day is for the physical being in the general context of how we humans function.

Therefore, there is the daytime to supplement your physical body with energy, to do all the things you must to get on with your life. Daytime supplements and supports your activities—it is a time for living.

As nighttime approaches, you are physically fatigued as your natural bodily rhythm tells you it is time to prepare for rest. Therefore, in Hoodoo the night is not for the living, instead, it is the time when the veil between the spirit realm and the physical world is lifted. Therefore, nighttime is when the dead awaken. A time for spirits to enter the world of the living.

This concept is very significant in Cemetary Hoodoo where conjurers visit graveyards at night. You will learn more about that as we delve into aspects of cemetery Hoodoo.

The Right and Left Hand of Conjure

Remember I told you Hoodoo was all about 'balance', no matter how powerful a conjurer is they must always maintain a balance between good and bad. The Left and Right Hands of conjure exist to define that balance.

Right-Hand work refers to the conjurer's work to bring about prosperity, blessings, healings, a change of situation, and the opening of new doors leading to better prospects for believers. This work is achieved in combination with a spiritual connection to the ancestors, and the power of rootwork.

Examples of daily Right-Hand rituals you can indulge in include sweeping your house from the back to the front. You do this to drive out negativity and the influence of any evil your home may be under.

Another one is to make offerings at crossroads. The offering can be made by dropping a few coins at the crossroad; it is a good practice to have some change handy when traveling. This act appeases the spirits of the crossroads and in doing so you are making sure the doors of opportunity remain open to you.

Cleanse your spiritual aura by asking for protection from your Black-American ancestors. They can work to make sure spiritual influences remain good for you and any bad residue is removed.

Reciting psalms from the Bible is another way to guarantee blessings and protection for yourself. You can recite these prayers while sweeping your home as a cleansing ritual.

The Left Hand in Hoodoo refers to the use of the practice for causing damage, vengeance, and ill health, but not entirely in that context. Using Left Hand Hoodoo to cause mischief is often a result of reversing any mischief that has been caused to the seeker.

Let's say a person has been put under a curse by an enemy who wants to see his downfall. A rootworker upon reading the seeker's condition will be able to identify the type of hex put and will proceed to reverse the curse which is how Left Hand Hoodoo works. Reversing the curse and transferring it to the person who wished it on the seeker is often done as a form of justice and revenge. Therefore Left Hand work must not be classified as dark Hoodoo, it is merely taking care of business and ensuring the safety of the seeker.

Spiritual Cleansing

Cleansing is another aspect of Hoodoo you must learn about. Seeking a cure for illness or a bad situation, or influence in life can be overcome through the process of cleansing or spiritual baths. This practice is common in many cultures and countries across the world. In Hoodoo a series of cleansing baths are prescribed to be followed by the believer. Scented crystals are added to the water and offer various curative powers. You will find a range of scented crystals sold at spiritual stores for treating various situations.

To perform a spiritual cleansing the crystals are dissolved in a tub of water or pail which is then poured over the body. While doing so you can recite or try manifesting your desires and wishes or say a prayer or read a psalm from the Bible. Psalms 51 for cleansing and 91 for protection are often recited during a cleansing procedure.

Scented crystals are even used in mop water for cleansing the house of impurities and negative forces. Or as a magnet for attracting good luck and positive energy, the crystals will be dissolved and used to wash clothes.

The use of minerals in cleansing is one of the basic practices of Hoodoo and is a part of the African and European cultures adopted into the practice.

Running water is considered the purest form of water for cleansing; a fine example of how important cleansing is is the ritual of baptism started by John the Baptist who offered people deliverance from their sins through a cleanse in the River Jordan.

Minerals, roots, tree bark, salt, and herbs are often used as material for spiritual baths. If you are purchasing crystals from a spiritual store they will be labeled for different purposes.

Cleansing can be used for removing what is called 'foot track magic' in Hoodoo. A practice brought over by Hoodoo's African ancestors, the spell can be used for good or bad.

During the process of working this magic, a concoction of roots, grave dirt, etc. is laid across the path of the person you are working the magic on. Once trampled the magic enters their body and will start to manifest the desired results the foot track magic is expected to offer.

When foot track magic is used for evil, where goopher dust is often a part of the ingredients, it has the power to bring negativity to the person's life and body.

Often when foot track magic is used against a person, it is with dark intentions, intended to bring about sickness and death, or crossing, hot-footing, and banishment.

A popular spell for attracting good luck and obtaining your goals is the Crown of Success Spell. People sitting for exams or having an important meeting or interview for a job they desire, seek out the power of this spell. Having a cleansing bath using Crown of Success oil will attract good luck and positivity.

Some popular crystals are those used for love potions and for protection. Here are the most used types of Hoodoo crystals.

- Pyrite—this stone is often added to a mojo bag or cleansing ritual as a means of attracting good luck and prosperity.
- Magnetite which is a type of naturally occurring magnet also called Lodestone—is a popular crystal for deflecting the evil eye. A Lodestone will offer

protection from hexes and will even strengthen the power of other materials used in the spell.
- Black Tourmaline—offers protection, this stone is good for empowering a person with self-confidence. This stone will also help to negate the power of negative or evil energies aimed at you.
- Rose Quartz—pink is an important color in Hoodoo, and Rose Quartz is the main crystal used for love charms.

Understanding Root Work

To be successful in the craft and practice real Hoodoo, you must understand how to work a root, to do so you must make that all-important connection with the spirits of your ancestors; embrace your heritage.

Rootwork, where the entire plant is used for conjure, was created out of the belief that spirits reside in the trees, plants, animals, soil, rain, lightning, and minerals.

Roots connect you with the creator, therefore in Hoodoo, we believe that roots are a primal power, connecting us to the force that created the universe.

It is from where Hoodoo draws its power. These elements found in nature are your connection between the spirit world and the physical world. Spirits reside in the roots therefore, harnessing their power will help you to create a change by asking the spirits to work between realms and grant what you seek. Unlike the physical man, spirits are able to travel between realms, initiating change.

Each root has a specific spirit assigned to it. Each plant defined by its flowers, seeds, and roots will be used for specific purposes

You must open up a portal between the two realities, yours

and the supernatural. When the spirits of a specific root you are using to obtain a favor, work on that need, there is a mirroring of that change between the two realms, making your desires a reality. Maybe to get a promotion in your job, win the love of someone, etc.

The spirits of the roots will work with you to open new pathways at the crossroads of life. These doorways which were blocked become open once you have begun to work with roots. Listed below are some popular roots used for performing various tricks.

Powerful Spirit Places

A spirited place in Hoodoo is a location where there is a convergence of spirits. The most favorable of these places are the spots where the residing spirits willingly work to aid the work of the conjurer. Some places will be more powerful than others if it is a kind of hub for conducting spiritual ceremonies.

For example, if a particular crossroad is often used as an altar by rootworkers, the number of good spirits dwelling there and willing to help increases. Hence, it becomes an almost sacred place for performing all sorts of Hoodoo rituals. Next, I will tell you about some of the most significant spirit places that are an important aspect of the craft.

Spirits

Before you begin seeking the help of spirits you must make an effort to understand the spirits. The closest spirits to you are those of your ancestors. I will explain further about making a connection with them. It is only once you have connected with the spirits of your ancestors must you reach out to other spirits.

These spirits are all around us. As I told you before, each

root belongs to a certain spirit and you must get thoroughly familiar with the workings of a root before you try to harness its power. Spend time learning about roots, their parts, and their various functions.

You must develop a deep respect for these spirits, including those of your ancestors. Offering up daily prayers and gifts is the best way to honor them and show them your respect.

Always work with spirits on a basis of giving and take. Never take from a spirit without giving something in return. Because the gift or favor you were offered can just as easily be reversed. Now let's move on to the most powerful places to make contact with spirits.

The Crossroads

In Hoodoo, quite similar to most religions, crossroads are a place of power, a land that does not belong to any man or realm. Crossroads are an altar where offerings are made and new paths are opened.

There you will find a doorway between your world and that of the spirit. Understand that many spirits reside at crossroads. It is there that you follow your destiny or path in life by opening up blocks that are stopping you from reaching the goal you desire.

You will work with spirits on a basis of giving and taking.

You must make an offering—a gift—in return for the favor you ask. Keep in mind that the 'give-and-take' policy must be adhered to because spirits if not properly compensated will take back whatever favor it is they granted. Therefore, a visit to the crossroads must be made with a proper offering. A vessel containing a photo of yourself together with biological parts of your body such as a bit of hair, toenail, or fingernail clippings, as well as sugar, and red palm oil, are often added. This offering is then buried while performing traditional crossroad offerings which is to indulge in a smoke or a drink of whiskey.

For example, if you were to work on a Hoodoo love mojo, such as the "follow me boy spell" the blend of ingredients to create the root, and make the boy you desire return your affections, would need to be buried at every intersection/crossroad leading from your house to his.

If you are working a hex though such as a "crossing spell", the discarded material would be left in the cemetery. These hexes are created to turn good luck into bad, to induce spiritual hostility, and for vengeance. Other times the used tools would be thrown into running water, that is if you are working on a spell to get away from a situation.

Crossroads are also used to discard used tools. Burnt candle wax, water leftover from a ritual, ashes from burning incense, etc. This waste is thrown to a side of the crossroads, after which the believer walks away without looking back.

Conjurers learned to improvise, and where there was no easy access to a crossroad, an artificial one was created. A circle would be drawn with a large X inside indicating the four corners of the crossroad. This image would be called a crossmark or even simply an 'X'. Scented powders called sachet (sashay) powders are used to draw the cross, either on the floor or on a made-up altar. I will explain more about Hoodoo powders in chapter three.

Sometimes the mark would be totally invisible and indicated with just five dots to symbolize the four roads and meeting points. This type of made-up crossroad would not be called the X. Instead, you will hear the names five-spot, cosmogram, or quincunx. The five-spot crossroad will not be used for disposing of spells, it serves more as an altar for fixing spells.

Offerings will be kept on each 'dot'; the type of objects placed on the dots will depend on the spell.

The main point to understand when it comes to the crossroads alter is that it is one of the vessels through which you will be able to manifest the power of roots enabling you to make a connection and harness the power of change by connecting the physical and spiritual world.

Cemetery Hoodoo, Graveyard Spirits, and Working Tricks

The type of spirits present at a cemetery are varied, plus, the potency of a graveyard is considered to be very high when seeking to perform a Hoodoo trick. Cemetery Hoodoo can be practiced for good and for bad; remember that Left-Hand Hoodoo must be used for the greater good only, as a defense, retaliation, and getting back at someone but never as a way of merely performing black magic with evil intent. Therefore, cemetery Hoodoo must be performed with that all-important 'balance' in mind.

Cemetery conjure can be practiced for blessings or for invoking a terrible curse on someone. However to do either you must first gain experience on how Hoodoo functions, more importantly, develop an open relationship with the spirits.

Graveyards function on many different levels in Hoodoo.

- They are the burial grounds for your ancestors and a good place to create a connection and offer prayers as part of connecting with your heritage.
- A cemetery is a place where you can find a crossroad to

set up an altar to make your offerings to the spirits.
- It is home to many different types of spirits, from different backgrounds and different religions coexisting. Therefore, it is a good place to make your spiritual connection.

A cemetery is a place of open principles in the sense that it is a place devoid of labels. Religion, race, or social standing in life do not matter there, the only common factor is death. Death is inevitable for us all and therefore, not to be feared. Keep this factor in mind and you will be able to make strong connections with the spirits of the graveyard.

Graveyards represent a place of rest, a hub of tranquility that is not affected by the chaos of the modern world. Hence it is a place of reflection for you to find solitude and peace to practice the craft. A cemetery will give you more access to spirits than any other place, it is a marvelous meeting point for the dead and the living to connect. It is also a station through which other spirits will pass through, giving you a chance to make a connection with spirits and entities of different levels. Think of a cemetery as a symbolic gateway. A point from which the living and the dead can cross interconnect.

Graveyard dirt is a potent ingredient for use in spells and is an important ingredient for making Goofer dust. It is particularly powerful when used for creating counter curses or reversing work done to you by another party.

When gathering cemetery dirt it is important to have a deep spiritual connection with the spirit giving you the dirt. Through the cemetery soil, the spirit will gain direct access to you and the work you are performing, therefore, it is important to make a proper connection and understand the nature of the spirit you are dealing with. Ensuring you develop a healthy connection with the spirit you are dealing with is important for the success of your work and will decide whether the work you perform turns out to be positive or negative.

You must perceive a cemetery as follows.

- A place of rest and tranquility for the dead and the living.
- A place to communicate with the dead
- A place to work

In Hoodoo we consider the cemetery, crossroads, and places of flowing water to be the most potent, powerful places. Graveyards have been blessed with prayer, they are sanctified grounds where the dead can lay at rest. To access the spirits there you must learn to listen, it is only then that you will begin to realize that the spirits have been talking to you all this time. To start your graveyard work you must first lay the groundwork. Introduce yourself to the spirits and let them judge you and decide for themselves (because the spirits are very similar to living in that aspect) whether they like you or not.

Therefore, it is important to follow certain etiquette when visiting a cemetery.

- Start to make regular visits to the cemetery as a sort of introduction. But never visit empty-handed. That is rude. You must appease the gatekeeper, typically the spirit from the first grave you encounter at the entrance.
- Take along an offering that you can drop at the entrance. A sort of gift for the doorman. Traditional offerings include candy, whiskey, cigars, cigarettes, baked goods, apples, herbs (make sure not to include

ingredients used in banishment spells), and of course the all-time favorite coins; they are goodies rootworkers have identified as favorites the spirits enjoy.
- Try to find gravesites that are over 100 years or close to it. Graves that have not been disturbed for long periods of time are best to conduct your work at, as it is rude to disturb recent graves, which will in turn upset the loved ones of the person buried there.
- You must never take anything out of the cemetery until the spirits have given you permission to do so. The cemetery is a very humbling place, therefore make sure to pay the highest respect to the spirits there as you are seeking their help and not vice-versa.

Once you have made your entrance offering you can walk into the cemetery. Often a rootworker will shield their faces when entering a cemetery because, as you know spirits talk, and if there is a conjurer already working with spirits in that particular cemetery, chances are your visit could be revealed to them if the spirits recognize you; Hoodoo magic works best when shielded from outsiders, therefore try your best to keep your identity hidden from spirits you are not working with.

A common practice when entering the graveyard is to walk in backward or have a cloth thrown across the face, even your palms acting as a shield will do. This is merely to shield your identity from the spirits who may be having a working connection with other conjurers from revealing your presence to them. It is therefore a practice reserved for only when you visit the graveyard for conjure work and not for when you are attending a funeral. Once your work at the cemetery is done do not leave without offering a gracious "thank you" to the spirits.

Leave your work when done and walk away without a backward glance, this gesture establishes trust; trust that your work is going to be successful. Remember Lot's wife, from the book of Genesis in the Bible, who turned into a pillar of salt as she looked back at Sodom and Gomorrah as they burned. Looking back symbolizes doubt, be strong and believe in yourself for the magic to work.

How to Make a Connection With Spirits—Divination

The closest and strongest relationship you will develop among the spirits will be the ones you form with your ancestors. They are family and will be your best allies helping you to carry out your conjure work. But make sure to appease your ancestors, as I told you before, the practice of Hoodoo begins with laying the groundwork, and starting with ancestor veneration on a daily basis is important for you to develop credibility as a rootworker, among your ancestors and the spirit world. Remember this tie is the most important in rootwork. If you recall I explained to you how every part of a root is inhabited by a specific spirit, therefore the strength of your spiritual connection will be the key to your success.

Keep in mind the cemetery can be dangerous if you are a novice, and trying to dabble with the spirit world in a cemetery before you are properly experienced can lead to you becoming the victim of a malicious spirit.

Therefore, the safest voyage into the spirit world as a rookie Hoodooist is to start making a connection with your ancestor's spirits. Establish an altar to them, nothing elaborate is needed; a candle, a few pictures if you have them and a bowl of water will be fine. Add the names of your dear departed relatives on a piece of paper to the altar. You can make daily offerings of candy, alcohol, or any of their favorite food.

Light the candle and offer daily blessings to your ancestors, talk to them and listen; through consistency and patience, you will be able to make a connection. It is a timely process, but eventually, you will make a connection.

Physically hearing them may take time, instead, you will feel certain vibes, and develop sudden cravings for food or alcohol which is how your ancestors let you know what they want. You may be able to see them in your dreams and talk to them. And eventually, you will begin to physically hear their voices—it is quite a shock at first, but remain calm and you will soon become familiar with their voices. Once you establish a strong connection with the spirits of your ancestors, you can visit the cemetery to broaden your experience of connecting with spirits of different temperaments, characteristics, wisdom, and also intent, which can be good or bad.

Spirits of the Cemetery

Do not expect to make a connection with a spirit on your first visit to the cemetery. You must first introduce yourself and allow the spirits to evaluate you. Some may be interested and some may just ignore you altogether, while others may try to trick you into gaining from you with no intention of returning any favors.

Absorb the solitude of the place and teach yourself to sense and listen. Walk around pausing around the graves, see if you feel a vibe, if you don't move on and if you do hang around longer to make sure you feel a connection. Once you do establish a feeling that connects you to the grave, observe the names on the tombstone. Take your information home and try to find out what you can about the people buried there. Knowing, if possible, their nature and character when they were alive will help you to establish if the spirit calling out to you has good intentions or bad.

In time you are bound to make a stronger connection with a spirit who is interested in getting to know you better and helping you with your work.

Open your mind and senses so you can feel the spirit trying to communicate with you. Get in tune with the vibes; if you feel fear, or dread it is best not to make a connection with that spirit; otherwise, feelings of joy or positivity will indicate a good spirit that is trying to communicate with you. Keeping yourself sensitive to these vibes is important to establish a proper connection.

Once you make the connection, treat your new friendship like any other. Start by getting acquainted with your new spirit friend. Do not get down to business immediately. That is rude. Plus, you can't go around asking spirits you barely know for favors.

Taking along the usual offerings will help seal the friendship, as you start to discover more about your spirit friend. Cultivate that friendship just as you would one with a living person, and plan regular meetings to keep the connection. Once you feel you have built a solid relationship and you are assured of the spirit's intentions to help, you can ask them for help with some of your work.

Precautions to Follow at a Cemetary—Cleansing Rituals, Take Back No Parasites

As described above your experience at the cemetery is not going to be an all rosy-cozy relationship with a kind spirit. There are many dangers to heed.

One important factor to keep in mind is to be consistent. You may have to make many visits to the graveyard, and take along many offerings or gifts before you even begin to make a connection with a spirit there.

Don't let the excitement of finally making a connection with the spirit world blind you to the dangers. Not all spirits are good, and some will try to trick you and cause harm. One way to discern the nature of spirits is to be attuned to the vibes you get off them, as I said before if you feel dread, anger or fear leave those spirits alone, but sometimes those spirits may not leave you alone.

There are malicious spirits who are hungry for a change of scene, they are looking for a free ride and you would look like the perfect vessel to walk out of the cemetery in. You can prevent an unwelcome spirit from latching onto you by performing a cleansing ritual.

In the section on cleansing, you learned about using crystal powder in baths as a form of spiritual cleansing. That is exactly what you must practice following a visit to the graveyard.

- You could take home, unknowingly, a parasitic spirit that has attached itself to you. This spirit will feed off your power and cause all sorts of problems. A cleansing ritual after leaving the cemetery will ensure this does not happen.
- You may have accidentally messed with some other rootworkers' work. Therefore, you could fall victim to whatever the intention of that work was. Again a cleansing ritual on leaving the cemetery will ensure the work does not manifest itself in you.
- Do not enter the cemetery to conduct your work decked up in any jewelry that can fall off. Leaving behind your personal effects will give spirits access to you, as they can form a connection with you through the jewelry.
- Do not wear open-toe shoes or any type of footwear

that will cause graveyard dirt to be tracked back to your home. That dirt in your home will become a portal for an evil spirit to follow you back.
- Likewise, it is customary to cover your head when entering the cemetery, now I told you to do this to avoid recognition, but covering your head serves another purpose, the head is believed to be a gateway into your body, and when left exposed a spirit can use it to enter. Additionally, you can rub some Florida Water on your forehead to act as a protective barrier.

A temporary cleanse can be done once you leave the cemetery to be followed by a proper spiritual cleanse once you get home. Florida Water is effective when mixed with salt crystals. You can rub the mix from your head to your toes cleansing yourself and pushing out any unwelcome presence that may have latched on to you.

Once home, you can use the same ingredients added to a tub of bathwater or in a bucket which you can use to pour over your head, thus washing out the negativities.

What is Florida Water?
It is neither water nor does it come from Florida. This liquid is a kind of mildly scented cologne made from a base of alcohol. In the olden days, citrus and lavender were the main scents used, although the ingredients will vary in Florida Water made today. The name Florida is a derivation of the Spanish word florido which means 'floral' probably as an indication of what the contents smell. Florida water is often used for protection and for attracting good luck to yourself as well as your home or place of work.

Harnessing the Power of the Cemetery
The power that you will find in a cemetery is turbulent, it can veer between both positive and negative energies. That is

why you must only approach graveyard conjuring once you have gained some experience in conversing and dealing with spirits and after you have increased your knowledge of Hoodoo and how best to protect yourself or block unwelcome forces.

The type of vibe you feel at the cemetery will differ from grave to grave. The power emanating from the grave of a person who met a violent or suffering death will be different from that of some who lived content and happy life. There are frustrations, anger, sadness, evil, and boredom to deal with when attempting to get the help of cemetery spirits.

Some spirits will agree to help you with your rootwork to bring about good luck, protection and wealth, etc. While some spirits will eagerly assist you with casting a lethal curse on someone.

Becoming a seasoned conjurer who can navigate the cemetery takes a lot of time and practice, therefore don't be in a hurry to practice conjuring at the graveyard because getting your work wrong can have dire consequences.

You can, however, harness the immense wealth of knowledge found at a graveyard. The place is home to spirits from all walks of life, people who have dealt with all types of situations in life, and ghosts who have learned more in death. Therefore, you have access to an immeasurable amount of knowledge that you can learn to harness to improve your life and help others. One of the most potent ingredients to take out of a cemetery is dirt from a grave. This root is full of potent power and can help enhance the work you are doing together with the combined help of the spirit from whose grave you took the dirt.

Manifesting a Love Spell With Graveyard Dirt

This is a simple trick to work, you will need Valerian root as well as dirt from the grave of a person who showed you affection. Mix the two ingredients together and find a way to sprinkle the powder on the personal belongings of the person you love; clothes, or shoes are ideal.

Protection for Your Home

You will need dirt from the grave of a spirit you have a good relationship with. Take that dirt and combine it with equal amounts of salt which you must then sprinkle around the windows and doorways, as well as the surroundings of your home to create a powerful barrier of protection.

Drive Away an Enemy

The spell you create to drive away someone with graveyard dirt is a lot more potent than when you use the Hot Foot Powder. You will need to collect dirt from the grave of an unprincipled person. Collect the dirt from where the heart would be, and mix the soil with sulfur and red pepper. You can tie it up in a red pouch and bury that mojo bag in a corner of the person's garden, make sure to choose the eastern edge to do so.

Using graveyard dirt to drive away someone is a very strong spell. Because of the strong power found within a cemetery, the spell can cause incredible harm to the person, in addition to driving them away, therefore, keep in mind the rules of Hoodoo and maintain a balance when practicing Left-Hand work. Revenge should only be sought out when absolutely necessary and justified.

Create a Mojo Hand of Prosperity

You will need to find the grave of a person who was prosperous in life. Quite often a conjurer will seek out the grave of someone who was a successful businessman, or a banker. The most important work of this spell is establishing a relationship with the spirit of the chosen person. Remember you need the permission of the grave's spirit to take away the dirt. The spell works in combination with other ingredients.

- Orange peel symbolizes prosperity.
- Cloves or black-eyed peas symbolize luck and new pathways.
- Fingernail clippings
- Pennies and silver coins

Add everything to a small pouch and ask for permission from the spirit to carry out your work, once you receive it, dig a hole and put in the coins. You can pour in some whiskey as an offering too, as a way to sweeten the deal. Then drop in the bag and close up the hole. Dig it out after seven days and you can then wear the mojo bag like a magnet for good luck blessed by the spirits of the dead. When digging up the hand make sure to give the spirit there another gift.

Hoodoo Dirt

Conjure draws its power from the Earth. The trees, the leaves, animals, water, and dirt. Grounding all this and creating a connection is the soil of the land—dirt. Therefore, in Hoodoo dirt holds immense power. It is where the dead are buried and therefore contains the power of the spirits.

Dirt is from where new life sprouts; rivers, and streams make their way through paths created by dirt, it is the foundation on which we build our homes, and the ground on which we grow our food.

The earth contains within it the cycle of life from birth to death and is the most powerful tool in conjure absorbing the power of the living and spiritual world. The earth beneath our feet connects us to all other tools—the crossroads, roots, and graveyard.

In Hoodoo we believe that our ancestors empower the earth. Their bodies have decayed and become one with the land from which new life springs. Therefore, they live again in the trees, plants, and water. Therefore the dirt of your land is your divine connection to your heritage.

You too will return to feed the earth just as your ancestors do therefore the power of the earth is boundless. And harnessing that power whether it is graveyard dirt or dirt from a crossroad, or your own backyard, you are using the essence of your ancestors to work your conjure.

CHAPTER 4
MATERIAL USED IN HOODOO

You have learned about places, spirits, and roots. In addition to these important aspects of Hoodoo, there are staple tools that every root worker must have around. These ingredients must always be a part of your stock as they play an important role in just about every work.

In this chapter, you will learn about the important material used in Hoodoo Conjure. The significance of each tool and how they influence your work.

Hoodoo Candles

The staple of all tools used when working on a trick is the candle. It is the beacon of light that paves the way for the rest of the work to be done. In Hoodoo the candle represents light and an illuminated path. It is a guide to show you the way, enlightening your path to guide you in the right direction.

Candles can be fixed to work a certain spell or they can be lit as an offering to the spirits. Candles have been used in ancient religions since the beginning. Candles have represented spiritual and magical beliefs in Roman, Egyptian, and Mediterranean cultures.

Candles are often one of the chosen tools among beginner Hoodooists. There are many tricks to be performed with candles, plus they are cheap; making them the ideal choice for learners.

A candle in Hoodoo serves many purposes; it can be used to illuminate the path for those seeking a special favor or the help of a spirit, it can be used to get rid of or burn obstacles and it can be used for casting spells.

While a seasoned rootworker will dress and fix candles with magical ingredients, to serve a specific purpose, you can easily purchase pre-loaded candles from your spiritual shop. Pre-loaded candles are those which have been imbibed with the power of enchanted oils, roots, and herbs.

In Hoodoo we use candles for many reasons, you can burn a candle with an intention attached to it, and as that candle burns your needs are communicated to the universe. In other words, your requests are sent across to the realm of the spirit world. The roots used to dress the candles will let the spirits know your desires so they can set about manifesting what you seek.

Candles are also used as offerings to spirits. They appease the spirit's appetite by feeding it smoke and light which spirits desire.

The popularity of candles only increased after the end of the Civil War, before that slaves did not have access to them as they were expensive, used only on the big plantations and slaves only had access to lanterns as a means of illumination. However, once African-Americans started to move to urban areas, Hoodoo took a turn and as you already learned, opened up a huge market of commercially produced Hoodoo tools. This is when candles received a huge boost. There were color-coded candles and enchanted candles to choose from. Candles that are already fixed to perform a required task are available at spiritual shops for you to purchase, making them the easiest

Hoodoo tool to try and master.

Terms Given to Hoodoo Candles

Before you visit a spiritual shop to purchase candles you must know the terminology attached to them.

- Fixed Candles

A fixed candle is one that has been dressed with roots and oils as well as blessed with prayers and intentions. Fixed candles are larger than the average type of Hoodoo candle and will come in a glass case. The candle's function will be printed on the front making it easy for you to choose. For example, the Money Draw candle will have its purpose displayed on the front and all you are required to do is light the candle at an altar and offer up prayers.

- Dressed Candles

Very similar to the Fixed Candle, this one means that the candle has been dressed with a specific root and oil to manifest what you desire. For example, if you are looking for a windfall and change in your monetary situation the candle can be 'dressed' with some Money Draw oil to manifest your desires. Since this candle is only 'dressed' you will have to 'fix' with prayers and intention when performing your ritual.

- Loaded Candles

They are just as the name suggests, loaded. The candles are hollowed out to facilitate oils and roots which can be thrust directly into the wax. The potency of the candle is believed to increase this way. If you are considering loading a candle thus, make sure to pick up a thicker stemmed candle so it does not crack.

- Rolled Candles

A candle that has been rolled in special oils and then in herbs is called a rolled candle. They are similar to the loaded candle, except the roots are stuck to the outside of the candle.

The Meaning of Colored Candles

Colored candles are not a part of Hoodoo culture. At the start candles were not even accessible to the slaves, leave alone color-coded ones. Simple candles were used and they were dressed with the intention of the rootworker.

However, we do live in modern times with candles freely available and in a variety of hues. Therefore, modern Hoodooist, and especially beginners like you will find that color-coded candles are very useful for staying focused on your intentions.

Color Coding for Candles

- Black candles—burn this when working a protection spell or when you are fixing a hex on someone.
- White candles—although used for healing and obtaining blessings, a white candle can be used for performing any kind of conjure because white is neutral and the first type of candle used by your ancestors for performing Hoodoo magic. You can dress the candle with your intentions.
- Pink candles—in Hoodoo pink symbolizes love. Burn a pink candle for happiness in your home and for spiritual healing.Red candles—this is a powerful color and represents your lifeblood. A red candle will be used for manifesting strength and courage, as well as for intentions such as love and attraction.
- Orange candles—represent success, energy, and clarity.
- Green candles—this candle is lit with the intention of wealth and good luck. If you are seeking success in your

job or future career offering your intentions through a lit green candle will help.
- Gold/Yellow candles—this candle is lit when a sudden change is desired. It is also lit for drawing good fortune.
- Blue candles—the power of this candle is a reflection of its tranquil color. Light one when you are trying to manifest joy, peace, happiness, and harmony within your life or home.
- Gray/Silver candles—they are lit for protection, or when you are working to banish an evil influence.
- Purple candles—to take control of a situation, maybe to turn tables at work or in your life.
- Brown candles—are quite appropriately colored, they are lit when seeking to win a court case.

You will also come across candles that have two colors. They are specially lit when you are working to reverse a particular situation.

- Black and white candles—these can be lit when you are working to reverse a curse/hex that has been put on you.
- Red and black candles—light one when you are working to reverse the evil influence of a person or spirit over your life.
- Green and black candles—are lit when you are working to reverse the financial difficulties that you are under.
- Red, white and green candles—offer triple blessings. When lit they offer you luck to draw money toward you, find love, and get rid of evil influences in your life.

Reading the Candle Flames

Reading a candle as it burns is something seasoned conjurers are able to do, it is not easy as the physical properties of a candle will change. How fast it burns, etc.

depends on the quality of the candle.

The flame of a candle can be interpreted in the following manner.

- A flame that jumps up and down—if you see this in the candle you have lit, it could indicate the presence of spirits who are trying to reach out to you. A jumping flame could also indicate a warning. Deciphering the meaning will depend on your interpretation and intuition given to the situation you lit the candle for.
- A steady flame—when the flame burns tall and unmoving it is an indication the magic you are working on is going ahead as planned.
- A dancing flame—this is when the flames move around, back and forth in all directions. It is an indication of good energy but that energy is not focused. When you see this, you must try making your intentions clear to the spirit the candle represents.
- Tall flame—when you see the flame rise up it is an indication of good energy and that your intentions are going to manifest real soon. However, a tall flame also indicates that those fast achieved results will not last long.
- A small flame—indicates the energy flow is limited and your work will take longer to achieve. You can try refocusing and making your intention clearer.
- A blue flame—you will see the blue at the bottom of the flame, and it indicates your work is going to yield positive results.
- A crackling, popping, or a hissing flame—of course, this means only one thing, you have spirits that are trying to contact you.
- A green flame—if you see this then expect prosperity,

especially if your intentions are for luck, success, and wealth.
- Black smoke puffs coming from the flame—is a sign that you have someone doing rootwork against you, it could mean you are under the influence of a spirit or conjurer.
- White puffs of smoke—will tell you that the work you are doing is progressing well.

Getting Started With Candle Work

Candles are a good first to start your work on Hoodoo conjure. They are cheap and you don't necessarily have to dress the candle, so you don't have to run out and purchase Hoodoo conjure oils. You can use a normal white candle for this purpose.

Start by holding the candle in both your hands and praying very clearly for your intention. Focus and think of the change you want and its outcome. Let's say you desperately want a promotion in your workplace. Make that intention clear, imagine getting that promotion and the positive change it will bring into your life. Focus on how you will be given the promotion, recognition of the productive work you have been doing, the salary increment that will be offered to compensate for the promotion, and the contributions you are making at your workplace.

Once you have made your intention clear to the spirits, (and not the candle, it is merely the vessel of transfer) place it in a safe place and light the candle. Stare into the flame and again make your intention very clear. Remember you are communicating to the spirits, and it is important to let them know the change you desire. Once you have made your intention clear, you can clear your mind and let the candle burn down.

Once it has burned down it indicates the transfer of your intention from the physical world to the spirit world where the spirits can get to work manifesting your desires.

Newcomers should start candle work simply. If you wish to dress or fix your candle, don't go out and buy a ready-made one. Purchase the Hoodoo conjure oils and roots and dress the candle yourself, ensuring you have a deeper spiritual connection to the entire work.

Water and Important Conduit in Hoodoo

In Hoodoo water plays an important part, it is the path that helps the spirits travel—the conduit. Placing a glass of water on the altar as you pray to the spirits will act as a doorway through which the spirits are able to enter the physical world. Therefore water is always present in a ritual.

Water is also the made ingredient for cleansing spells, it holds the power to wash away and cleanse you of any unwelcome influences. In spiritual practices, water symbolizes new beginnings, healing, and energy.

Rivers in Hoodoo are highly symbolic. They are places where many spirits reside and are important meeting places, similar to crossroads. It is a place of renewal, a vessel through which you can get rid of evil influences and perform cleansing rituals. The river can be used to renew your soul and indicates new beginnings. Baptisms are performed in rivers so the person receiving a cleanse can wash away their impurities and those impurities are then taken away by the flowing water.

Roots

Roots are another important material in Hoodoo and should be kept on hand to conduct your work. While you can purchase roots from a spiritual shop, you will also find many growing around your home and in the woods. Roots can be stored and dried in bunches, in jars, and as powders. Different roots have different effects and depend on the spirit that dwells within them.

The Devil's Shoestring

Among all the interesting names Hoodoo has awarded to roots, the Devil's Shoestring is probably the most appropriate. This root is a staple in protection spells as well as conjure work to invoke good luck.

Using the Devil's Shoestring is used to trip up the devil and evil work. Three types of roots belonging to the Honeysuckle plant genre (also a powerful plant used for binding spells) are used to make this root. It is widely believed that the Devil's Shoestring is a root the African slaves picked up from the native Red Indians who were held as slaves together with the people of Africa.

The three types of plans from which the roots are obtained include:

- Viburnum Alnifolium also called Hobble Bush found in Canada and the northern parts of the US.
- Viburnum Opulus, better known as the American Cranberry Bush although it is not really a type of cranberry. This plant too grows in the north and in Canada.
- Viburnum Prunifolium, popularly called Blackhaw. This is the only variety of Devils Shoestring which can be found growing in the southern states of the US and is therefore believed to be the original Devils Shoestring used by the slaves on the Southern plantations.

All three plants have long, flexible, and tangled-up roots making them perfect for tripping up evil. Learn about its uses in mojo bags as good luck spells that you can have when seeking wealth and advancement in your workplace.

There are many other types of plants too which are available under the same name, and often used for conjure work such as Devil's Shoestring. But ask any seasoned rootworker and they will tell you to not deviate from the original list of plants given above if you expect positive results.

Roots and Their Power

The number of roots and botanicals used in Hoodoo is wide. Each root serving a specific need will have the power to influence unique situations.

The Calamus Root

This influential root is also called Sweet Flag. A rootworker will offer this charm to a believer who seeks to gain control over a particular situation or even a person. Therefore, the Calamus root is often used in spells created for empowerment. Examples include the Follow Me Boy spell, commanding spells, and commanding spells. Calamus roots are used in conjure bags with a mix of other potent ingredients in case someone wishes to dominate or take control of a situation. Likewise, the root chips can be dried and burnt as incense when charming other talismans such as candles.

The Angelica Root

This powerful root has many names; the Archangel Root, Holy Ghost Root, and Dong Quai. The Angelica root is used in conjuring to empower women and as a protector and tool for healing. It is also a good luck charm for households and when dealing with health issues; the root is also believed to ward off evil influences. Placing the root in different colored pouches and combining it with various ingredients such as oils and flowers will offer diverse results.

High John the Conqueror Root

This is one of the main roots used by conjurers for working tricks. The High John the Conqueror root is used for manifesting all sorts of situations. Its main power lies in the ability to manipulate your luck, improve your love life, and for purposes of justice. In the olden days, the John the Conqueror root was worn by slaves seeking protection from the slave minders. High John the Conqueror Root was a symbol of power for the African slaves who used it to fight back, there are several stories that lead to the background of the root centered on a cunning slave a trickster who managed to manipulate his slow-minded masters.

Today, you can buy the root packaged according to size, there are even male and female roots you can decide to use depending on the type of trick you are planning on working on. The root can be worn whole on your body or added to mojo bags; it is available to buy whole, or as chips, powder, and oil. John the Conqueror Root, High John the Conqueror, Low John the Conker, and High John are some of the names the root is associated with.

Salep Root/Helping Hand Root/Lucky Hand Root

This root is carried by people seeking luck in gambling and games. Working the roots magic will yield good luck and fortunes. Therefore, it is often carried in a mojo bag by people seeking luck in games of chance. The name helping hand is a suggestion of how the root works—helping people who require sleight of hand to garner winning. Combine an entire Helping Hand Root with Five Finger Grass inside a red-colored flannel bag to attract money.

Five Finger Grass

Also called Cincoenrama or Cinquefoil, Five Finger Grass is a type of herb. In Hoodoo the plant is used for its magical powers. The five points of the leaf represent wisdom, love, money, health, and power. The herb is added to mojo bags or burned to invoke good luck and improve self-confidence.

Various parts of the plant are used for its curative powers against fever and diarrhea. In Hoodoo the herb is used for success, to empower your hands to work magic to bring you luck. The root is also used to manipulate others to come to your aid.

Dixie John Root

Another name for this root is Southern John or Beth Root. In Hoodoo conjure this root invokes blessings for prosperous family life, and improves one's sexual relationship and love. The root can be boiled and drunk as tea for improving your love life or added to the wash cycle of your bed sheets if you seek an improvement in your sex life.

Valerian Root

Also called Vandal Root is used at times as a replacement for graveyard dirt. It is a potent ingredient for manifesting peace within one's home, subduing quarrels, and also for darker tricks such as summoning demons.

Personal Material for Creating a Link

In Hoodoo working a change calls for your intentions to be clearly communicated. And in the case of a personal spell you are working on for yourself, another, or even a group of people, it is important to establish a strong and clear connection to the individual.

To establish this connection you will need to include personal effects. Popular material used for this purpose includes blood, sometimes menstrual blood, semen, worn and unwashed clothing, nail clippings, and bits of hair. By adding these personal items to your conjure work, you are including the essence of that individual in the work.

Additional material to establish the link can include a photograph and the full name of the person you are doing the conjure work on written on a piece of paper. Sometimes you may only have the name and a photograph to work with, keep in mind that working with these materials will not have as strong a connection as the personal items mentioned above.

Hoodoo Powders

The use of powders in Hoodoo is very much a part of the craft's Southern heritage. Blowing powder and sprinkling powder as a means of dispelling evil spirits, cleansing a place, and bringing in luck are practiced by several folk religions across the globe.

The use of blowing powders for powerful conjure work in the West Indies is common. Even in Asian nations such as the island of Sri Lanka, where the worship of the deities from nature is common, a traditional 'kattadiya' the local equivalent to rootworkers, will perform exorcisms or cures using smoke from burnt roots, drum beats, and the blowing of blessed powders in the face of victims to drive out demons.

There are many traditions Hoodoo conjurers followed in southern states, one is the sprinkling of blessed powder along the front step and in the four corners of one's house to keep out evil influences. Powders can be added to mojo bags to create good luck charms attracting love, money, good health, and power. Otherwise, powders can be added to dresser drawers to keep your clothes smelling good and for empowering the wearer with good luck.

Hoodoo powders are used in hexes and curse work too. Some can be used to drive a person away while others thrown on the doorstep or in the garden on one's enemy can attract bad luck to them and cause serious harm if the root worker so wishes.

The tradition of using powders in hoodoos is an old one, with roots in African, and European traditions. Towards the latter parts of the 19th century, the types of Conjure powder used began to change with scented powders offering various solutions for problems and being sold at spiritual stores. The powders are available as blowing and sprinkling sashay powders.

In the olden days though, before the commercialization of Hoodoo, powders were made with a mix of herbs, roots, and minerals. They remain among the most popular in use today.

- Magnetic Sand

This powder which is an extremely fine iron grit which is a powdered form of cast iron shot is meant to act as a magnet drawing luck to you. Therefore, it is popular among people seeking winnings in games of chance, those wanting to increase their finances, and for luck in love.

A powerful combination for using Magnetic Sand is to attach it to a Lodestone —explained in chapter 2. The general practice is to get hold of two Lodestones. One is perceived as male and one as female. You then sprinkle the magnetic sand on the stones, which is called feeding the he and feeding the she. Carrying these stones around in a small velvet mojo bag will attract money as well as luck in love.

- Sulfur Powder

Sulfur was a popular material used by rootworkers in the olden days for work against an enemy, known as Enemy Tricks. It is a type of naturally occurring mineral dust that is used in several tricks. A popular one is when the sulfur powder is mixed with salt and laid out in lines as a form of cleansing for a house. Or when it is sprinkled in a cross from across the footprint of an enemy.

- Salt powder

Salt has been a versatile and necessary mineral in Hoodoo conjure from the beginning. It is often used for purification rituals, blessings, and for protection from magical influences. Inherited from European folk religions is the practice of placing a pinch of salt in every corner of the room before the commencement of the ritual.

Salt can be added to red pepper, or sulfur if you are working on a particularly potent spell against your enemy, but if it is simple protection, just salt alone will work. The type of salt whether sea salt, table salt, or kosher salt doesn't really make a difference.

- Red pepper powder

A vital ingredient used by rootworkers working on Enemy Tricks, red pepper is often an ingredient in Hot Foot Powder, Goopher Dust, and Crossing Powder.

- Black pepper powder

Works similar to red pepper powder and will be used in creating trouble for an enemy in the areas of family, job, and finances. Another way to cause mischief for an enemy is to add a personal/biological part of the person you are jinxing to a bottle containing red pepper powder, black pepper powder, salt, and sulfur. Bury the bottle at the entrance of your enemy's front door so they walk over it on a daily basis.

With the commercialization of Hoodoo, close to the 20th century, powders were ready-made and available in spiritual stores. Some were mixed with talcum powder and emitted a pleasant fragrance so people would dab them on their person.

Popular ready-made powder mixes include hot foot powder, the Crown of Success spiritual powder, King Solomon Wisdom powder, Crossing Powder and look me over powder.

How to Use Hoodoo Powder

A very traditional method of sprinkling powder is to do so while walking backward. It is customary to take an odd number of steps backward. Ideally, 21–steps if you have the room, or anywhere between three and nine will suffice.

Other methods of sprinkling Hoodoo powder include:

- Blowing the dust in the direction of the person's house.
- Adding lines of small mounds of dust in corners of the house.
- Making a crossing pattern on the street for the enemy to walk over.
- Dressing candles with powder
- Dusting the powder on the personal items of the person you are working the trick on. Clothes, shoes, socks, and hankies are good choices.
- Blowing the powder in the four directions.

Dressing Items with Sachet/Sashay Powder

Dressing a candle with powder is often done once the candle has already been dressed with magic oil. A dab of oil over the powder is applied to create a potent dressing of double layers which some rootworkers believe increases the power of the candle.

You can also "dress paper" if they are important documents. When getting ready to send off any important documents out of which you are expecting favorable replies or outcomes, dress the paper with a dash of the crown of success powder.

Dip your fingers in the powder and gently run along the length of the paper from top to bottom.

You can even give it an added boost by burning the powder with incense and then letting the smoke waft over the paper. If you are submitting legal documents and fear any reprisal or are in search of a favorable outcome, use Court Case Powder to dress the papers.

When purchasing ready-made powders it is important to verify the authenticity of the brand you are purchasing the products from. Most powders don't actually contain the traditional ingredients required to make the powders a potent tool; even easy-to-obtain ingredients are not always included in those sashay powders.

Unless you plan to source every ingredient and make the powders yourself, make sure to purchase your ready-made ones from an authentic source.

Hoodoo Incense Powders

The use of incense in Hoodoo is old with direct links to traditional African religious practices as well as a part of Native American sacred rituals. Let's not forget the influence of Christianity too on the craft and the religious use of incense smoke to cleanse and bless a person and place.

Rootworkers who traditionally recite Psalms from the bible when doing a job will use incense as part of the ritual to anoint the work with smoke and bless the intentions they put forward to the spirit world, clearing the room of negativity and any unwelcome spirits.

During a job that is meant to affect a change in someone who is not present at the ritual, incense will be used as a form of transporter carrying the effects of the conjure through the smoke to the person the work is being done on.

There are also incense powders that are linked to specific zodiac signs and if a rootworker knows the zodiac sign of the person the trick is being performed on they will use that specific powder to make a stronger connection to the individual and ensure better success.

Incense is popular in conjure as a form of purification where mojo bags, talismans, and rootwork are 'smoked' by holding them over incense smoke to cleanse, purify and bless.

The Native Americans, from who the African slaves learned a lot about nature, herbs, and spirits of the Earth, favored incense made from tobacco and herbs such as cedar, yarrow, sweetgrass, and sage. Ceremonial pipes which are an important aspect of Native American traditions and culture were smoked with tobacco while smudge sticks were made from white sage as the popular choice.

Types of Incense to Choose From
If you like doing your conjure work the old-fashioned way you can choose from the types of natural herbs, flowers, tree resin, and wood-based incense powders. These are types of incense used from ancient times and will burn while giving off a pleasant and fragrant smell.

Sage is by far the most popular herb used for incense, while sandalwood, obtained from the sandalwood tree, is both a highly fragrant and a popular type of wood chip incense; it is also one of the more expensive types of wood chip incense sold.

Resin incense is made from the sap of trees, some well-known types include Frankincense and myrrh, which were even gifted to the infant Jesus on his birth. Copal, pine, and benzoin are other types of resin incense you can obtain.

How to Use Incense

You can add a small mound of self-burning incense to a fireproof dish or vessel and set the top of the mound on fire, once it lights, blow it out and let the embers burn to let off the smoke. Or you can use a charcoal disk on which to burn the incense. The charcoal disk must be held with tongs over a lit flame, you can use your stove for this, once it lights, adds it to an incense burner or a stone burner, and as it smolders drop the incense powder on top.

Use an incense burner to carry around in case you want to manipulate the flow of smoke in a particular direction. For example, you can choose a good luck incense such as Dragons Blood powder and light it at your front door allowing the smoke to waft inward thus encouraging good luck to flow into your home. You can even add good luck incense to the soil of a plant growing near your front door to attract good fortune to your home.

Incense Blends Used in Hoodoo Conjure

There are incense blends for various objectives that you can use. A visit to a spiritual shop will reveal a whole range aimed at achieving a specific purpose. Here is a guide on the types of incense powder available and the types of ingredients included in each mix.

- Unblocking and Clearing Incense

This incense powder is used to clear out blocks that may be stopping you from moving on with your life. Obstacles from the past that you find hard to move can be broken by lighting this incense. You can use this incense if you are constantly doubting yourself or feel a need to gain self-worth. Typical ingredients used are white sage, ylang-ylang oil, myrrh, cloves, lavender buds, and coriander seeds.

- Hot Foot Incense

Quite similar to oils and powders, Hot Foot Incense is used to get rid of someone. The incense contains a volatile mix of black pepper, cayenne, red chili, sulfur, etc. Therefore, this incense should not be burned inside your house, nor must it be inhaled by you or anyone else, the smoke is not meant for. The best method to make Hot Foot incense powder work is to light it outside, or in the vicinity of the house of the person, you are targeting.

- Love Attraction Incense

Always a popular choice whether it is oil, powders, mojo bags, or incense, Hoodoo tools aimed at improving one's love life will always be popular. Popular ingredients used in this incense include white sage, sandalwood oil, rose oil, rose petals, buds of lavender, and other herbs.

- Money Drawing Incense

This incense is used for invoking good luck and improving your finances. Burn the incense and let the smoke waft over your purse and wallet, as well as documents and other tools linked to your finances. Included in the incense powder are fenugreek, vetiver, cinnamon, alfalfa, and other herbs associated with good luck.

- Protect Me Incense Powder

This incense can be burned for protection. You can smoke the areas around the front, back and surroundings of your home to guard against unwelcome forces. The incense can be held inside your vehicle for protection and in general, can be used on a regular basis as a protection cover. Ingredients used to make the incense include geranium, myrrh, blessed thistle, St John's wort, cloves, essential oils, and other materials that enhance the power of spiritual protection.

- Uncrossing and Reversing Incense Powder

Burn this incense to rid yourself of any hex or curse you feel you may have been put under. Combining the burning of this incense with an uncrossing ritual will ensure better results. By using the uncross and reverse incense you are sending the curse back to your enemy. Included in the mix are powerful ingredients; angelica root, verbena, hyssop, peppermint, and calendula.

Magic Oils

Hoodoo oils are popular choices for dressing candles, bathwater, or roots. There are many names awarded to Hoodoo oils; dressing oils, formula oils, anointing oils and magic oils are some. The oils are a reflection of Hoodoo's beginnings and are derived from African, European, and Native American knowledge and beliefs.

The attributes of a plant included in magic oils are derived from its image; how the plant looks, its shape, and color influence what is believed to be its magical attributes. Therefore, oil is derived from.

The oils are aptly and simply named indicating exactly what the charmed oils are supposed to achieve.

For example, if you were seeking to do work on someone expecting them to bend to your will, you would need the Bend Over Oil. Or if you wanted to resolve a dispute or a problem you would need Uncrossing Oil. Likewise, Reconciliation oil will help you to solve issues with your lover. Then you get the Money Drawing Oil, Kiss Me Now Oil, and Hot Foot oil the latter of which you know is used to drive away someone by influencing the magic to work through the person's feet because they have trampled your hot foot charm.

Other oils that are popular include John the Conqueror Oil which is meant to improve male virility, and Van Van oils which is extremely popular and used to dismiss hexes, and enemy spells, to manifest luck, and to increase the potency of other ingredients used in talismans, and mojo bags.

Steady Work Oil will bless the user with steady work while Psychic Vision bestows the user with visionary dreams and prophecies.

Terminology for Using Magic Oils

- Anointing—this is when you would add one small drop of oil to your fingertip, and then place it on the forehead of the person you are 'anointing' with the oil, you can of course anoint yourself in a similar manner. The term anointing will refer to rubbing oils on the body.
- Dressing—rubbing just a minute amount of oil on a root, candle, money, important document, etc. for fixing the objects with an intention. It is the same as anointing, but you say 'dressing' because it is an inanimate object.
- Condition oils and Formula oils too refer to these same types of oil in combination. A dressing oil and anointing oil will be called a formula or condition oil with the exception that at times a condition oil would be more explicitly used for dressing objects. While formula oils will include anointing oils and other perfumed formulas which are used on the body.

The Use of Hoodoo Conjure Oils

There is no hard and fast rule to say that dressing oils are explicitly reserved to dress objects and anointing oils are only for anointing the body, they can be interchanged and used with no problem.

If you wanted to bring good luck and wealth into your life you would have to use magic oil to dress objects. People who seek good fortune in games of chance, cards, and the lottery will use oils such as Fast Luck oil, Money Drawing oil, Money Stay With Me oil, and Three Jacks and a King oil. You can dress the money you intend to use in the game with the oil for prosperous results.

When seeking luck in love, dressing a candle with Follow Me Boy Oil, Love Me oil, Come to Me oil, and also Van Van oil will yield the desired results if the intentions are clearly communicated to the spirits through the burning of the dressed candle.

How to Use Conjure Oils

- As always to dispel an evil force or ill effect that has been inflicted on the body, you must use conjure oils from head to toe. Uncrossing oils can be rubbed starting at the head and down the body to finish with the evil influence being rubbed out through the toes.
- To anoint oneself with good luck spells or love spells the process is reversed, in this case, you are trying to attract luck to yourself, therefore you start rubbing the oil from your toes and up your body, all the way to the head. Keep your intention strong while doing so, or you can get the help of a rootworker.
- Healing oil, King Solomon Wisdom oil is used only on the head. You must rub the oil with the fingertips of your dominant hand. Use only the thumb, index, and middle finger.

Mojo Bags

These little pouches have symbolized an aspect of Hoodoo almost from the birth of the craft. The discreet little pouches in which you can carry charmed roots, herbs, crystals, etc. are extremely popular among rootworkers. The combination of materials tied together in a mojo bag becomes profoundly powerful as they supplement each other. Thus, the trick you are working on, or even the jinx you wish to bestow on an enemy is potent when fixed to a mojo bag. You can even carry one around when seeking out luck and money in games of chance, when attending an important job interview and when meeting a particular love interest, or to stop a vicious strain of gossip.

The mojo bag will contain a mix of magical items that are a careful combination to offer what the seeker desires. The pouch must be worn close to the body, touching the skin for it to have the desired effect.

Mojo bags are called many names; gris-gris or Gris bags, hand, a bag of tricks, nation sack, flannel, and luck ball. Gris-gris is more popular in Louisiana and South Carolina where Hoodoo originated among the African slaves.

Red flannel is the preferred choice for a mojo bag. The name mojo is a derivation of the West African word for prayer—mojuba. To put it simply a mojo bag is a magic spell you can carry around, a prayer, a trick, that has been enhanced with your intention. Carrying one around reminds you of the change you are trying to make and functions under the placebo effect which is the power of suggestion.

The bag offers both psychological and spiritual support to your belief. Seeing the bag feeling it against your skin and knowing there is magically working into the contents there is a great way to stay empowered and positive toward your goals, which in turn works to manifest your desires.

It is your positive energy and belief in the power of each material included in the bag that feeds the magic, making it work. Therefore, before you put a mojo bag together it is important to fully understand the power within each of the roots, herbs, etc. added to the pouch.

Typical Ingredients That Are Added to a Mojo Bag

Plants, roots, minerals, crystals,s and animal parts are all used to create a mojo bag. Bones and teeth from animals are often used and dressed with a conjure oil.

Sticks, roots, dried berries, herbs, and other parts of a plant too will be included. Roots such as High John the Conqueror are popular choices for gris bags.

Lucky charms too are added when creating a mojo bag; they include rabbit's foot, four-leaf clovers, and items that belong to whoever the bag is intended for; they can be personal items such as pieces of jewelry, fingernail clippings, hair, etc. Silver coins too are often added to a mojo bag to improve its potency.

The combination of ingredients included in a mojo bag will depend on the spell you are working on.

If you were to make a gris-gris to attract love, you would place an Adam and Eve root together with the personal effects of the person you are trying to attract and dress the bag with Van Van oil.

While dressing the objects it is important to clearly visualize your intentions, and see them happening; thus, you will pass on your desire to the spirits that reside in the objects there. Seal the spell by lighting a pink candle dressed in a dab of Van Van oil as you prepare for the magic to take place.

If you have offered to make a mojo bag for a friend, keep happy and kind thoughts of the person in your mind as you put the bag together, infuse the charm with plenty of good vibes to make the spell work and the spirits look upon your friend with favor.

Consider the preparation of the bag a form of ritual; prepare a candle, pink for love, green for prosperity if you are making a mojo bag for attracting money. Purple candles if you are trying to battle a disruptive or difficult colleague spreading rumors about you at work. Choose the candle according to the work you are doing, dress it with the appropriate oil and then place your intentions at the altar.

The Number of Objects Allowed in a Mojo Bag

Hoodoo is based a lot on superstition as you would have learned by now. From anointing your body with oil, to cleansing and walking into a cemetery, superstition plays an important role.

When putting a mojo bag together it is important to keep track of the number of items. They must always add up to an uneven number. But the number of ingredients must be a minimum of three and a maximum of thirteen. You must count the personal items you added to the bag as part of the odd number you are trying to achieve.

Once all the objects are inside you may want to dress the bag with oil or sometimes whiskey as you would when burying a mojo bag on a gravesite.

Phases of the Moon for Conducting Successful Rituals

There are some conjurers who believe the phases of the moon have special effects on the creation of a mojo bag. Let's look at a few.

- When Lunar Energy is at its Height—Full Moon

Symbolizes the moon in full strength. And is particularly

empowering for mojo bags created for fertility, love, healing, prosperity, and reaching success in your goals.

- A Time for Dispelling Dark Conjure—Waning Moon

The two-week period from which the full moon starts to diminish in size is called the waning moon. Use this period to destroy curses and hexes cast on you or someone seeking your help. Create mojo bags for dispelling hexes, removing curses, overcoming obstacles, and solving problems.

- A period of Low Energy—Dark Moon

This is the phase when the illuminated face of the moon is turned away from the Earth and toward the sun. During this phase, the moon is hardly visible to us on Earth and its power is at its lowest. Due to low lunar energy at this time do not create mojo bags, instead spend the time which lasts for about three days in prayer, offering up your intentions to an altar on which you have lit a dressed candle.

- The Birth of a New Cycle—New Moon

The moon is still not visible to us on Earth, but it has started its transition from the new moon phase to the waxing phase. Which is the new phase you must prepare to start making your mojo bags. The new moon is an ideal time for creating mojo bags with the intention of manifesting new beginnings such as seeking a new love, changing jobs, or starting a new business.

- Lunar Energy Starts to Increase—Waxing Moon

This is the two-week period between the transition of the new moon to a full moon. This time is conducive to creating mojo bags with the intention of improving one's creativity, prosperity, health, and bonds in relationships.

The Color of a Mojo Bag Makes a Difference

In the olden days, gris bags were made with red flannel, however, just like the color-coded candles that empower us psychologically, today there are colors awarded to mojo bags depending on the conjure work you are aiming to achieve.

Mojo bags can also be empowered with minerals to increase their potency, they too change according to the color of the bag and the spell that is being cast. Here is a list of mojo bag colors, and the type of conjure work associated with each color.

- Blue

This color is associated with creating a calm effect in the body, it promotes serenity, and healing and increases the power of intuition. Gris bags made for healing, safe travels, and bringing about peace are made in this color.

- Black

This is considered a powerful color and therefore used for diffusing black magic. Mojo bags to reverse curses, made for protection, to dispel negativity, for justice, for vengeance, and for challenging the truth to come out are made in black.

- Brown

Represents the earth, the dirt which holds the power of the ancestors, and the power of death and birth. Brown is a humble color, it also symbolizes stability and reliability. You can use brown mojo bags to create spells for family prosperity and stability, the health of your pets, and peace within the home.

- Gold

This color symbolizes wealth and prosperity and is

considered a potent color imbibed with lots of energy. Use gold to make mojo bags for success in your business, attracting good fortune, and reaching your goals.

- Green

Symbolizes new beginnings—spring, and prosperity. Use this color to create mojo bags for manifesting good luck, hope, healing, growth, achieving goals, prosperity, and changing the direction of your life.

- Red

Often the chosen color for creating mojo bags, red symbolizes the life force within us. The color also represents warnings, love, and passion. Therefore, you can use a red mojo bag for casting spells related to energy, passion, sexuality, and courage.

Making a Mojo Bag

Creating a mojo bag is a ritual, and depending on how careful you are with your conduct the potency of your spells will grow or diminish.

Create an altar for yourself before you lay out the material that goes into the gris bag. You can create an altar, if you don't already have one, by purifying a work table. Wipe it down with a mixture of salt and sulfur to cleanse the area of any impurities.

Place a candle and dress it with the appropriate conjure oil. Once done you can lay out the objects you have chosen to include in your gris bag. Light the candle and make your intentions clear, focus and let the spirits there see what you wish to achieve.

If you are not making the gris bag for yourself, placing a photograph of the person you are making the bag for will help you to focus your intention on them, thus letting the spirits too know about the person for who their help is required.

Concentrate on your intention as you start adding each item, remember to stick to an odd number. As you place each item in the bag you must thank the forces contained there. The spirit of the roots, the spirit in the crystal, the herb, and so on. While doing so never lose sight of your intention, concentrate on it right throughout, and let your thoughts wash over each object as you pick it up and place it in the bag.

While placing the objects in the bag you can recite your intentions out loud or read a psalm or prayer. It's up to you, it is not necessary to say it out loud if you are not comfortable, reciting the prayer or intention in your mind is good enough. Remember your main objective is to make your intention for creating the mojo bag clear to the spirits so they can begin to work the magic and initiate change on the spiritual plane.

Once done pull the strings and close the bag, thank the spirits for their assistance and burn any names you may have written down on paper with the flame of the candle.

Gris bags should be made with good intentions, remember the rule of Hoodoo where Left-Hand conjure is only practiced as a necessity and never as an indulgence. You must not go around cursing or hexing people just because they crossed your path, there must be a valid reason for putting a hex on someone, such as vengeance or getting back at someone for the pain they caused you. But never as an indulgence—keep in mind that whatever you put out to the forces of the spirit world will come back to you threefold, therefore, set the pace for only good returns. Hoodoo is about maintaining a balance between good and bad.

CHAPTER 5
HOODOO SPELLS

A spell is a process of manifesting your intentions. For a spell to be successful it is important to focus on your intentions and make them clear, you must be specific about what you desire.

Remember your Hoodoo spells are working through the spiritual realm, through spirits who have come to your aid, and they need proper instructions in order to manifest your exact desires.

If you are casting a love spell, they must know the details. Are you looking for a new love, do you want an old love back, or do you want to improve an existing love affair?

Making your intentions clear will ensure the end result of the spells is satisfactory and not one you wish to undo with the greatest urgency.

Most importantly you must maintain that all-important balance between good and bad when casting a spell. Every desire you manifest through magic will come with its own string of consequences—a domino effect of change. Therefore, you must be prepared to face the challenges together with the gifts you are granted. Never take the casting of spells lightly, it is simply not a case of changing one path; your actions will of course set off a series of changes that will affect your life, and that of others connected to the change you initiate through conjure.

Casting Spells in Hoodoo

Spellcasting in Hoodoo is based on repeating your intentions as you dress and anointing each of the objects you will be using. Some conjurers will resort to repeating their intentions over and over while others will focus their minds on projecting their intentions to the objects that are being used while reciting psalms from the Bible.

Either method is acceptable provided you focus on projecting your intentions clearly. This can be done through careful repetitions of what you wish to achieve.

Choose a quiet time of the day to start your spell casting, and make sure the room you choose is free from outside noise and disturbances. Start your prayers, and psalms and focus on your intentions from the moment you start gathering the tools you will be using in the spell. Remember it can be said as a chant or verse, although chanting is not a popular method for casting spells in Hoodoo, you say it out loud or you repeat it in your mind, either way if your intentions are clear the spirits will hear them.

Reading of the Scripture When Casting Spells

Reading verses from the Bible or reciting psalms is most often practiced by rootworkers during the casting of spells. Here are some popular options.

Psalm 91 for Jinxes

This verse is read three times over when anointing a candle during a ritual to undo a curse of jinx.

Psalm 91: He that dwelleth in the secret place of the most High shall abide under the shadow of the Almighty.

2 I will say of the Lord, He is my refuge and my fortress: my God; in him will I trust.

3 Surely he shall deliver thee from the snare of the fowler, and from the noisome pestilence.

4 He shall cover thee with his feathers, and under his wings shalt thou trust: his truth shall be thy shield and buckler.

5 Thou shalt not be afraid for the terror by night; nor for the arrow that flieth by day;

6 Nor for the pestilence that walketh in darkness; nor for the destruction that wasteth at noonday.

7 A thousand shall fall at thy side, and ten thousand at thy right hand; but it shall not come nigh thee.

8 Only with thine eyes shalt thou behold and see the reward of the wicked.

9 Because thou hast made the Lord, which is my refuge, even the most High, thy habitation;

10 There shall no evil befall thee, neither shall any plague come nigh thy dwelling.

11 For he shall give his angels charge over thee, to keep thee in all thy ways.

12 They shall bear thee up in their hands, lest thou dash thy foot against a stone.

13 Thou shalt tread upon the lion and adder: the young lion and the dragon shalt thou trample under feet.

14 Because he hath set his love upon me, therefore will I deliver him: I will set him on high, because he hath known my name.

15 He shall call upon me, and I will answer him: I will be with him in trouble; I will deliver him, and honor him.

16 With long life will I satisfy him, and show him my salvation. (psalm 91, 2015)

Psalm 51 and 108 For Cleansing

Use this prayer for cleansing and keeping evil away from yourself and your home. Repeat the psalms three times over while making the cleansing water which you can dab on your head, back of the neck and chest/heart, hands, and feet (the significance of each of these points I have explained below).

To make the cleansing water you will need the following items.

- One glass of water
- Half bottle of Florida Water
- One candle
- Holy water which you can obtain from the church. You will find a holy water font at the entrance of the church. Or check the baptistry which will be located at the back of the church. Or you can check your spiritual supplies store.
- Purification incense powder such as Dragons Blood or Frankincense oil.

First, light the candle and make your intentions clear. You will need half of the Florida Water in the bottle, to that add the incense or the Frankincense oil, and then top it up with the Holy water. Shake the bottle to combine all the ingredients.

Once done reciting the psalms, one at a time, three times over, after which you can anoint yourself with the water.

Psalm 51: Have mercy upon me, O God, according to thy

lovingkindness: according unto the multitude of thy tender mercies blot out my transgressions.

2 Wash me thoroughly from mine iniquity, and cleanse me from my sin.

3 For I acknowledge my transgressions: and my sin is ever before me.

4 Against thee, thee only, have I sinned, and done this evil in thy sight: that thou mightest be justified when thou speakest, and be clear when thou judgest.

5 Behold, I was shapen in iniquity; and in sin did my mother conceive me.

6 Behold, thou desirest truth in the inward parts: and in the hidden part thou shalt make me to know wisdom.

7 Purge me with hyssop, and I shall be clean: wash me, and I shall be whiter than snow.

8 Make me to hear joy and gladness; that the bones which thou hast broken may rejoice.

9 Hide thy face from my sins, and blot out all mine iniquities.

10 Create in me a clean heart, O God; and renew a right spirit within me.

11 Cast me not away from thy presence; and take not thy holy spirit from me.

12 Restore unto me the joy of thy salvation; and uphold me with thy free spirit.

13 Then will I teach transgressors thy ways; and sinners shall be converted unto thee.

14 Deliver me from bloodguiltiness, O God, thou God of my salvation: and my tongue shall sing aloud of thy righteousness.

15 O Lord, open thou my lips; and my mouth shall show forth thy praise.

16 For thou desirest not sacrifice; else would I give it: thou delightest not in burnt offering.

17 The sacrifices of God are a broken spirit: a broken and a contrite heart, O God, thou wilt not despise.

18 Do good in thy good pleasure unto Zion: build thou the walls of Jerusalem.

19 Then shalt thou be pleased with the sacrifices of righteousness, with burnt offering and whole burnt offering: then shall they offer bullocks upon thine altar (psalm 51, n.d.).

Psalm 108: O God, my heart is fixed; I will sing and give praise, even with my glory.

2 Awake, psaltery and harp: I myself will awake early.

3 I will praise thee, O Lord, among the people: and I will sing praises unto thee among the nations.

4 For thy mercy is great above the heavens: and thy truth reacheth unto the clouds.

5 Be thou exalted, O God, above the heavens: and thy glory above all the earth;

6 That thy beloved may be delivered: save with thy right hand, and answer me.

7 God hath spoken in his holiness; I will rejoice, I will divide Shechem, and mete out the valley of Succoth.

8 Gilead is mine; Manasseh is mine; Ephraim also is the strength of mine head; Judah is my lawgiver;

9 Moab is my washpot; over Edom will I cast out my shoe; over Philistia will I triumph.

10 Who will bring me into the strong city? who will lead me into Edom?

11 Wilt not thou, O God, who hast cast us off? and wilt not thou, O God, go forth with our hosts?

12 Give us help from trouble: for vain is the help of man.

13 Through God we shall do valiantly: for he it is that shall tread down our enemies (psalm108, n.d.).

Psalm 118 for Creating a Prosperity Bundle

The psalm is recited over the offerings gathered to make a mojo bag of sorts for prosperity. This tiny pouch/packet containing the charms can be kept in your wallet next to your money to ensure a continuous flow of cash.

You will need the following:

- Water in a glass
- A money note(one dollar will do)
- 1. Candle
- 1. small sprig of thyme
- A small piece of orange peel
- Gold or green thread (the colors of prosperity)

Gather all your ingredients at an altar, light the candle which you can dress with Good Luck conjure oil and make your intentions very clear, while you thank the spirits that dwell within each of the pieces you are using for the spell.

Reciting Psalm 118 three times over, it is one of the popular prayers in Hoodoo for invoking prosperity and financial stability.

When you have finished the prayers, place the one-dollar bill face down, then place the orange peel and thyme over the bill and fold it up into a square. Use the thread to wrap up the bundle, you must twist the thread around the packet in inward motions—wrap the thread bringing it around toward yourself, because you are asking luck to enter your life, remember you would wrap the thread outwards if you were working on a spell to drive someone away. Once sealed you can carry the pack in your wallet next to your money. If you like you can hold incense smoke over the packet before putting it in your purse or wallet.

Psalm 118: O give thanks unto the Lord; for he is good: because his mercy endureth for ever.

14 The Lord is my strength and song, and is become my salvation.

15 The voice of rejoicing and salvation is in the tabernacles of the righteous: the right hand of the Lord doeth valiantly.

16 The right hand of the Lord is exalted: the right hand of the Lord doeth valiantly.

17 I shall not die, but live, and declare the works of the Lord.

18 The Lord hath chastened me sore: but he hath not given me over unto death.

19 Open to me the gates of righteousness: I will go into them, and I will praise the Lord:

20 This gate of the Lord, into which the righteous shall enter.

21 I will praise thee: for thou hast heard me, and art become my salvation.

22 The stone which the builders refused is become the head stone of the corner.

23 This is the Lord's doing; it is marvellous in our eyes.

24 This is the day which the Lord hath made; we will rejoice and be glad in it.

25 Save now, I beseech thee, O Lord: O Lord, I beseech thee, send now prosperity.

26 Blessed be he that cometh in the name of the Lord: we have blessed you out of the house of the Lord.

27 God is the Lord, which hath shewed us light: bind the sacrifice with cords, even unto the horns of the altar.

28 Thou art my God, and I will praise thee: thou art my God, I will exalt thee.

29 O give thanks unto the Lord; for he is good: for his mercy endureth for ever (psalm118, n.d.).

The Purpose of Anointing Certain Points of the Body

During cleansing or protection rituals or any other, that calls for anointing, there are specific parts of the body that need to be anointed. You must know the purpose behind this ritual in order to reap the full benefits of a conjure oil, blessed water, or powder you may be using.

- Anointing the Head

A person's spirit dwells within their head, therefore, it

must be cleaned regularly to ensure blessings, as well as to make sure any unwanted spiritual residue has not made its home there.

- Anointing the Back of the Neck

In Hoodoo this area is considered the most vulnerable in terms of the back of the neck being the most accessible place for spirits to enter your body. Safeguarding this entrance with protection oils and cleansing waters will ensure unwelcome forces do not gain access to your body.

- Anointing the Heart

The heart is your core, your center, and bears your anxieties, fears, and stress felt by your spirit. Therefore cleansing or protecting your heart through anointing rituals will ensure it remains pure and strong enough to face the burdens of life and ground you to remain on the right path of conjure.

- Anointing the Hands

Your hands are your tools, they can be weapons, used to destroy or they can bring comfort. Spirits use your hands to carry out the work they are entrusted to do. Your hands will help you carry out your physical activities and will help you to engage in your spiritual work.

- Anointing the Feet

Feet take you on your journey of life. They must be safeguarded to ensure you stay on the right path both physical and spiritual.

Working Hoodoo spells is not complicated. Apart from making your intentions clear and reciting the psalms or prayers, there are no long and complicated verses to recite.

Making sure you offer up thanks to your ancestors and the spirits of the roots is important. Maintaining a strong connection with your heritage, your ancestors, and the spiritual world will ensure you receive help for successfully working spells.

Casting Love Spells

Love spells are among the most popular in all magical crafts and folk religions. Love is a universal need. Therefore, when someone has the power to cast a spell and bend love to their command the temptation to manipulate another's affection is high.

When casting a love spell it is important to remember that taking matters into your own hands with regards to making a particular person bend to your will and love you, through conjure, will have repercussions that are not always pleasant. When you don't let the universe decide for you and you try to force the affections of a particular person who shows no interest in you, you are making yourself vulnerable to outside forces.

Often the person you choose to cast a spell on may not be the love of your life, they may not be the person you want to spend the rest of your life with. Therefore, it is best to let the universe decide and cast a love spell that brings love your way and not the affections of a particular person who would not be noticing you in a romantic context if not for the conjure work you did.

Conditions for Casting Hoodoo Love and Good Luck Spells

- You must choose the proper day for casting spells of luck to ensure the conjure has every chance at success in love and luck.
- When casting good luck and love spells it is always best

to seek out a full moon or waxing moon day which falls on a Thursday or a Sunday.
- Choose your candles accordingly. Green for prosperity, gold for riches, pink for love, and red for intense passion. Dress the candle in conjure oil choosing what's appropriate from those I have mentioned in chapter three.

Listed below are a few simple love spells you can start off with. Cast a spell for love to come your way, consider being open in your request, and work on a conjure for love and affection but leave it up to fate to decide on who that person should be.

A Quick and Popular Spell for Creating a Love Charm

You will need.

- A silver ring
- White cloth

Place the items on your altar and make your intentions very clear as you give thanks to the spirits and your ancestors. Ask for love to cross your path, but try and avoid asking for the love of a specific person who shows no interest in you. Let the universe and the spirits choose for you a better match.

Once you have made your intentions clear, wrap the ring in the white cloth. You can then dig a hole in the ground and bury the ring under the light of a full moon or a waxing moon. Offer the spirits a gift by pouring some wine over the cloth containing the ring and then cover up the hole and let the charm remain there for seven days, after which you can dig it up. Give thanks once more to the spirits and wear the ring to attract the love of your life.

Honey Jar Spell for Love

You can try casting a simple honey jar spell too as one of your first love spells. It is an ancient and very simple ritual that must be performed for seven days. Although the details of this spell are available online I will list it here for your ease.

- Dress a pink candle in Adam and Eve oil or an equivalent while concentrating on your intentions. Be very clear about what you want out of the spell, an old love back, the love of someone you adore, etc., and light the candle.
- On a piece of paper write the name of the person you desire three times, if you are casting a love spell to find love and not bend the will of someone specific you may write 'find my future husband', 'my perfect mate', etc.
- Flip over the paper and write your name three times on the back. Here again, make your intentions clear so the spirits hear you.
- Fill a jar with honey and place the paper inside making sure the tips of your finger touch the honey. Lick the honey from your fingers thinking of your intentions, being together with the one you desire.
- Seal the jar and hide it away from sight.
- Let the candle burn down and light one every week on the same day at the same time. You can burn the candle down or use a large seven-day candle for the spell.

Healing Spells

This is a quick healing spell for an injury or pain you can use to practice your power of concentration.

You will need a piece of fluorite, or if you can find one a very clear amethyst. Psalm 34 to read out.

If the pain is closer to your right hand, hold the stone in it, if it's left, then hold the stone in that hand. You can sit or lay down. Now focus very intently on what you want, healing from the pain you suffer. Imagine you can see a bright white light spooling out at the bottom of your feet.

Now, as you repeat psalm 34, take the stone and start from your feet, see yourself draw up that white light along your body. Pull it up toward your head, and let the light cover your body until it reaches your head. Now raise your hand with the stone in it above your head and see the light expand over you. Then draw the light down to the spot where you have the pain. Focus your energy on healing the pain there and continue to repeat psalm 34. Repeat the psalm three times and visualize yourself getting healed. Repeat the ritual as many times as needed and you will heal. How fast you do depends on your faith and concentration powers.

Psalm 34: I will extol the Lord at all times;

11 Come, my children, listen to me; I will teach you the fear of the Lord.

12 Whoever of you loves life and desires to see many good days,

13 keep your tongue from evil and your lips from telling lies.

14 Turn from evil and do good;

seek peace and pursue it.

15 The eyes of the Lord are on the righteous, and his ears are attentive to their cry;

16 But the face of the Lord is against those who do evil, to blot out their name from the earth.

17 The righteous cry out, and the Lord hears them; he delivers them from all their troubles.

18 The Lord is close to the brokenhearted and saves those who are crushed in spirit.

19 The righteous person may have many troubles, but the Lord delivers him from them all;

20 He protects all his bones, not one of them will be broken.

21 Evil will slay the wicked; the foes of the righteous will be condemned.

22 The Lord will rescue his servants; no one who takes refuge in him will be condemned.

Spell to Dispel the Evil Eye

The evil eye has a lot of influence and can affect believers and non-believers alike. It is generally born out of jealousy, or a deep-seated rage and a need to cause destruction or chaos in someone's life. A person may develop jealousy and hatred toward you merely because you have what they have been too lazy to achieve or simply lack the talent to do so. That anger, envy, and rage are all directed toward the other via the evil eye.

Protecting yourself from the evil eye and preventing its influence from entering your home can be done through the following ritual.

You will need.

- A glass of water
- One white candle
- Holy water
- Three Evil eye beads
- One Camphor cube

- Psalm 37

Place the glass on a table or altar you made, and light the candle while making your intention clear—to dispel all evil eye influence on yourself, your home, or anyone else on whose behalf you are performing the ritual.

Take the glass of water and some of the holy water to it, then the three evil eye beads, all the while keeping your intention clear. Then place the cube of camphor on top. This will float and offer its purification power to the water.

Once done you must start your prayer. Recite Psalm 37 three times over while stating your needs clearly.

Psalm 37:

26 Do not fret because of evil men or be envious of those who do wrong;

27 Turn from evil and do good; then you will dwell in the land forever.

28 For the LORD loves the just and will not forsake his faithful ones. They will be protected forever, but the offspring of the wicked will be cut off;

29 the righteous will inherit the land and dwell in it forever.

30 The mouth of the righteous man utters wisdom, and his tongue speaks what is just.

31 The law of his God is in his heart; his feet do not slip.

32 The wicked lie in wait for the righteous, seeking their very lives;

33 but the LORD will not leave them in their power or let them be condemned when brought to trial.

34 Wait for the LORD and keep his way. He will exalt you to inherit the land; when the wicked are cut off, you will see it.

35 I have seen a wicked and ruthless man flourishing like a green tree in its native soil,

36 but he soon passed away and was no more; though I looked for him, he could not be found.

37 Consider the blameless, observe the upright; there is a future for the man of peace.

38 But all sinners will be destroyed; the future of the wicked will be cut off.

39 The salvation of the righteous comes from the LORD; he is their stronghold in time of trouble.

40 The LORD helps them and delivers them; he delivers them from the wicked and saves them, because they take refuge in him.

Once done the charm or guard is now ready to protect you and your home from the evil eye. Place the glass at the entrance of your home, and make another for the rear entrance. This way your home and you will guard against the evil eye which when directed at you will get pulled into the water and drown.

You must refresh the glass of water every two weeks or as the water reduces. Top it up, take out the beads and clean them well and replace the cube of camphor.

Your talent for casting spells and conducting rituals of working conjure will only grow with your knowledge and understanding of the craft. Do not rush into any ritual or spell until you fully understand the consequences and what you will be dealing with.

Certain aspects of Hoodoo rituals can be dangerous to the foolish, it is by no means a craft to be taken merely for its ability to do 'magic'. It is a way of life and gift you will be bestowed by your ancestors as you honor and take care of their needs in the spiritual realm.

Continue to research and read as much as you can on the practice. Find an authentic root worker from whom you can learn about the ancient ways of Hoodoo. Always respect the power of spirits, maintain a relationship of giving and take and you can go on to reap the benefits of a healthy working relationship with Hoodoo.

CONCLUSIONS
THE MYTHS AND FACTS OF HOODOO

As you have now been initiated into the practice of Hoodoo, you already know its true nature. A folk art born out of a need for salvation, infused with the wisdom, culture, and magic of other ancient religions and ways of life.

At the heart of Hoodoo beats the roots of the African-American people, the wisdom of the land obtained from the Native Americans, and the beliefs and spirituality of the Christians.

It is a practice supported by your ancestors the slaves who suffered on Southern plantations, it is a craft held up by the spiritual world and it is in part a practice that borrows the faith and prayers of Christian teachings.

A practice of evil? A dark craft intent on causing harm?

Hoodoo never was and never will be that mythological practice created by the colonists, slave traders, and fame-hungry producers of Hollywood.

Voodoo never did and does not exist.

It is a corruption of the sacred religion of the Fon Nu people and those in Haiti. Vodou is a religion of power, respect, and devotion to the creators of the universe, the spirits of the land, and the people who enrich its ways.

You know the beginnings of these religions through which Hoodoo was born. You know the practice was not created for vengeance, nor was it used as such. Hoodoo was a protector, a tool used to fight back when necessary only, and to this day, that is the essence of the Hoodoo.

A Craft That Uses Both Hands

Hoodoo is a practice that requires the conjurer to practice magic with both hands, Right-Work and Left-Work, the two balance out each other keeping the equation between good and bad stable.

The practice of Hoodoo conjures, no matter how powerful one becomes, must always remain humble. You are only a vessel through which the spirits and your ancestors are allowed to conduct their work in the land of the living.

Your place is to seek them out and aid them to help you and those who need hope and pride to be brought back into their lives—just as Hoodoo did for your slave ancestors so many years ago.

Honor and respect are the cornerstones of Hoodoo, honoring the land that is energized by the power of your ancestors, giving thanks to the spirits, and carrying out the work of God through your own hands.

It is not your place to go about dispelling the myths surrounding Hoodoo, it is your place to safeguard the true nature of the practice which only a faithful rootworker will know.

Go to the crossroads and pray for new paths to be opened unto you. Use your connection with the spirit world to create a balance in your life and that of others who seek your help.

Live within the boundaries of Hoodoo and you will forever be blessed.

GLOSSARY

- Working tricks—root work that has been activated/set in motion, a spell.
- Divination—the practice of interacting with the spirit world.
- Reading-on—Conducting a reading on a person who is suspected to be under the trick of another conjurer
- Psalms—sacred songs or verses from the Bible
- Crossing—spells to cast to cause torment, counteract a jinx for revenge
- Hot footing—to get rid of someone, to cause them to depart.
- Banishment—a spell to get rid of something or someone
- Fixed—to dress or anoint (candle) tool used for a spell or ritual
- Smudge sticks—a bundle of herbs, roots of which the tips are set on fire, put out, and allowed to smolder allowing the purifying smoke to cleanse a room or person.

REFERENCES
AFRICAN HISTORY: EXPLORING THE AMAZING TIMELINE OF THE WORLD'S RICHEST CONTINENT – THE HISTORY, CULTURE, FOLKLORE, MYTHOLOGY & MORE OF AFRICA

African Pygmies: The world's shortest tribe. 2020. Hadithi. https://hadithi.africa/african-pygmies-the-worlds-shortest-tribe/
A Venda folktale. n.d. Tambani. http://tambani.co.za/venda-folktales/folktales-in-english/the-year-of-hunger-2/
Makaudze, G. 2013. It still makes sense!: Shona ngano (folktale) and the contemporary Zimbabwean socio-economic and cultural setup. International Journal of development and sustainability, 2(2), 521-529.
African Roots: The Nguni Tribe of Southern Africa. 2015. Genesis Magazine. https://genesismagz.com/southern-africas-largest-tribe-the-ngunis/
Ashton, N. 2013. Rwanda in Focus. Intercontinental Cry. https://intercontinentalcry.org/the-batwa-rwandas-invisible-people-19581/
Balyage, Y. 2000. Ethnicity and Ethic Conflict in the Great Lakes Region. Bugema University. https://opendocs.ids.ac.uk/opendocs/bitstream/handle/20.500.12413/4968/Balyage-MAK-Res.pdf?sequence=1
Batwa people and experience. 2021. Primate World Safaris. https://primateworldsafaris.com/the-batwa-people-experiences/
Batwa: The history and culture of a marginalized people in Central Africa. Unrepresented Nations and Peoples Organisation. https://unpo.org/article/19031
Beck, R. B. 2000. The history of South Africa. Greenwood Publishing Group.
Bewitched forests and waters of the VhaVenda (part 1). 2013. Van Hunks. http://www.vanhunks.com/lowveld1/venda1.html
Brian, F. 2005. Tribal Warfare and "Ethnic Conflict" Cultural Survival. https://www.newsweek.com/biologist-eo-wilson-why-humans-ants-need-tribe-64005
Bryant, A.T. 2010. The Stabbing of Shaka and Ndwandwe War that Led to the Movement of The Ngoni and Others From Zululand. Ngoni People. https://www.ngonipeople.com/2010/10/stabbing-of-shaka-and-ndwandwe-war-that.html
Chabururuka, N. 2019. Mwari the One God. The Patriot.

https://www.thepatriot.co.zw/feature/mwari-the-one-god/

Chacha. n.d. What to Know About Zulu People, Their Culture and Tradition. Answers Africa. https://answersafrica.com/what-to-know-about-the-zulu-people-their-culture-and-tradition.html

Choi, C. 2009. The Final Days of Homo erectus. Inside Science. https://www.insidescience.org/news/final-days-homo-erectus

Cief Dingiswayo. n.d. SA History. https://sahistory.org.za/people/chief-dingiswayo

Cirjak, A. 2020. What Was The Original Name Of Africa? World Atlas. https://www.worldatlas.com/articles/what-was-the-original-name-of-africa.html

Clemence, M., & Chimininge, U. 2015. Totem, Taboos and sacred places: An analysis of Karanga people's environmental conservation and management practices. Int J Humanit Soc Sci Invent, 14(11), 7-12.

DeBeer, J. n.d. Camelthorn Giants. Bushman Stories. http://www.bushmenstories.co.za/

Dunham, W. 2014. Knuckle Sandwich: Did fFst Fights Drive Evolution of Human Face? Reuters. https://www.reuters.com/article/us-science-face-idUSKBN0EK1OD20140609

Eric. 2021. Pygmies Now an Endangered Hominid Species in Africa: Bantu Expansion Threatens Their Existence. Human Evolution News. https://subspecieist.com/indigenous-tribes/pygmies-bantu/

Flank, L. 2015. Shaka Zulu: The Real Story. Hidden Stories. https://lflank.wordpress.com/2015/07/31/shaka-zulu-the-real-story/

Flemming, E. 2020. What was pre-colonial Africa. Sid Martin Bio. https://www.sidmartinbio.org/what-was-pre-colonial-africa

From Butwa to Mthwakazi: Celebrating history, culture. 2019. The Patriot. https://www.thepatriot.co.zw/old_posts/from-butwa-to-mthwakazi-celebrating-history-culture

Gee, H. 2021 How Homo erectus Was, and Was Not, Like Modern-Day Humans. Literary Hub. https://lithub.com/how-homo-erectus-was-and-was-not-like-modern-day-humans

Giama, C. 2016. The Surprisingly sticky Tale of the Hadza and the Honey Guide Bird. Atlas Obscura. https://www.atlasobscura.com/articles/the-surprisingly-sticky-tale-of-the-hadza-and-the-honeyguide-bird

Gillis, D. H. 1999. The Kingdom of Swaziland: Studies in political history (No. 37). Greenwood Publishing Group.

Guenther, M. G. 1999. Tricksters and trancers: Bushman religion and society. Indiana University Press.

Hadza social-organization. n.d. Exploring Africa. https://www.exploring-africa.com/en/tanzania/hadzabe/hadza-social-organisation

Hamilton, D. L. 1996. The Mind of Mankind: Human Imagination, the Source of Mankind's Tremendous Power. Suna Press.

http://novan.info/ant.htm

Hayzed. n.d. A Lesson for Everyone (Swaziland Folk Tale). Quote. https://www.quotev.com/story/7654275/Folktales-around-the-world/10

Henderson, J, S. 1930. The South-Eastern Bantu. Cambridge University Press.

History of Great Zimbabwe. 2014. The Herald. https://www.herald.co.zw/history-of-great-zimbabwe/

Husseinali, N. 2013. Hadza 4: Exploring the Lifestyle. Word Press. https://moizhusein.wordpress.com/2013/01/02/hadza-4-exploring-the-lifestyle/

Ian. 2021. Batwa "Pygmies": History and Present. Experts Gorilla Highlands. https://experts.gorillahighlands.com/daily-dose/2021/05/17/batwa-pygmies-history-and-present

Jardin, X. 2009. What Became of Neanderthals? We Ate 'em, Made 'em into Jewelry, Says Scientist. Boing Boing. https://boingboing.net/2009/05/18/what-became-of-neand.html

Kora. n.d. SA History Online. https://www.sahistory.org.za/article/kora

Kwekudee. 2013. Batwa People: One of the First People on Earth and the Original Inhabitants of Great Lakes Region in East Africa Before The Bantus Arrival. Trip Down Memory Lane. https://kwekudee-tripdownmemorylane.blogspot.com/2013/03/batwa-people-one-of-first-people-on.html

Kwekudee. 2014. Ewondo (Yaunde) People: The original Inhabitants of Yaounde, The Capital of Cameroon. A Trip Down Memory Lane. https://kwekudee-tripdownmemorylane.blogspot.com/2014/09/ewondo-yaunde-people-original.html

Ladz. 2016. How the Khoikhoi Society Was Organized Political Organization. Mubula History. https://mubulahistory.blogspot.com/2016/12/how-khoikhoi-society-was-organized.html

Lederle, G. 2014. Hunting with the Hadza. Africa Geographic Stories.https://africageographic.com/stories/hunting-with-the-hadza

Lewis, J. 2002. Forest hunter-gatherers and their world: a study of the Mbendjele Yaka pygmies of Congo-Brazzaville and their secular and religious activities and representations (Doctoral dissertation, University of London).

Lewis-Williams, J. D. (2018). Three nineteenth-century Southern African San myths: a study in meaning. Africa, 88(1), 138-159.

Little, B. 2021. How Did Humans Evolve? History. https://www.history.com/news/humans-evolution-neanderthals-denisovans

Lutz, M. 2005. The Bantu Languages. Bulletin of the School of Oriental

and African Studies, 68 (3). S0041977X05490278.
Lwanga-Lunyiigo, S. (1976). The Bantu Problem Reconsidered. Current Anthropology, 17(2), 282–286. http://www.jstor.org/stable/2741540
Madenge. 2021. The Hadza Tribe: History, Culture, Religion, Myths. United Republic of Tanzania. https://unitedrepublicoftanzania.com/the-people-of-tanzania/daily-life-in-tanzania-and-social-customs/major-tanzania-ethnic-groups/how-many-tanzania-tribes-biggest/the-hadza-tribe-history-culture-religion-myths-people-population-dna-baboon-hunting-gatherers-david-choe-women-culture-bushmen-hadzabe/#Hadza_Tribe_History
Maringozen. 2022. Zwide KaLanga The Great King Of The Ndwandwes Who Created Mfecane Wars In The Southern Africa. Opera News. https://za.opera.news/za/en/culture/50f210af883c2d7a432a1f75837e4cba
Mbuti Pygmies. n.d. Anthropology Research. https://anthropology.iresearchnet.com/mbuti-pygmies
McCleland, D. 2019. Port Elizabeth of Yore: The Khoi and San – The First Inhabitants. The Casual Observer. http://thecasualobserver.co.za/port-elizabeth-yore-khoi-san-first-inhabitants
Mcginnis, B, C. 2017. African Tribalism. Penn State. https://sites.psu.edu/global/2017/04/19/african-tribalism
McKie, R. 2009. How Neanderthals Met a Grisly Fate: Devoured by Humans. The Guardian. https://www.theguardian.com/science/2009/may/17/neanderthals-cannibalism-anthropological-sciences-journal
Mpepereki, S. 2014. Tracing the Shona Back to the Great Lakes Part 3. The Patriot. https://www.thepatriot.co.zw/old_posts/tracing-the-shona-back-to-the-great-lakes-part-three
Mvenene, J. 2020. A History of the abaThembu People from Earliest Times to 1920. African Sun Media.
Ndlovu, R. 2021. Venda People Culture and Language. Buzz Feed. https://buzzsouthafrica.com/venda-people-culture-and-language-2
Nicolaides, A. 2011. Early Portuguese imperialism: Using the Jesuits in the Mutapa Empire of Zimbabwe. International Journal of Peace and Development Studies, 2(4), 132-137.
Nurse, G. (1973). Ndandwe and the Nguni. The Society of Malawi Journal, 26(1), 7–14. http://www.jstor.org/stable/29778286
Oluach, R. 2020.The History of The Great Changamire Dombo. Africa OTR. https://africaotr.com/the-history-of-the-great-changamire-dombo
Patou-Mathis, M. 2020. The Origins of Violence. Unesco. https://en.unesco.org/courier/2020-1/origins-violence
Pearce, D. G., Lewis-Williams, J. D., & Pearce, D. G. 2004. San spirituality:

roots, expression, and social consequences. Rowman Altamira.

Peires, J. B. 1982. The house of Phalo: a history of the Xhosa people in the days of their independence. Univ of California Press.

Penn, A. 2019. Homo Sapiens and Neanderthals: Did They Mate? Battle? Both?. Shortform. https://www.shortform.com/blog/homosapiens-and-neanderthals

Pontzer, H. 2012. Overview of Hominin Evolution. Knowledge project. https://www.nature.com/scitable/knowledge/library/overview-of-hominin-evolution-89010983

Power, C. 2015. Hadza gender rituals—epeme and maitoko—considered as counterparts. Hunter Gatherer Research, 1(3), 333-359.

Press News Agency. 2021. What Drove Homo Erectus Out of Africa. Press News Agency. https://pressnewsagency.org/what-drove-homo-erectus-out-of-africa/

Pygmies. n.d. Yaden Africa. http://www.yaden-africa.com/the-culture/tribes/pygmies

Pygmy peoples: Ethnic group of center africa. n.d. Native Breed. https://www.nativebreed.org/pygmy-peoples-ethnic-group-of-center-africa

Rigby, N. 1994. Tall tales, short stories: The fiction of Epeli Hau'ofa. World Literature Today, 68(1), 49-52.

Rimmer, L. n.d. Prehistoric Empires – The Geographic Ranges of 5 Human Species. Abroad in the Yard. https://www.abroadintheyard.com/prehistoric-empires-geographic-ranges-human-species

Rogers, K. n.d. The expansion of the Bantu out of western Africa and the eradication of the indigenous peoples of central and southern Africa. Doc Droid. https://www.docdroid.net/Hc2nulc/bantu-expansion-eradication-pygmies-khiosan-pdf

San. n.d. Siyabonga Africa. https://www.krugerpark.co.za/africa_bushmen.html

Schoeman, S. 1987. Settlement in South Africa: Early migrants and the Nguni. Africa Insight, 17(3), 192-198.

Shangaan Tsonga. n.d. Kruger Park. https://www.krugerpark.co.za/africa_shangaan_tsonga.html

Smillie, s. 2019. The Lost History of the Griqua. New Frame. https://www.newframe.com/the-lost-history-of-the-griqua

Smith, A. 2020. Interesting Things That are Most Recognized About the Culture of the Xhosa People. Buzz South Africa. https://buzzsouthafrica.com/xhosa-people-tradition-and-dance

Stapleton, T. J. (2006). Faku: rulership and colonialism in the Mpondo Kingdom (c. 1780-1867). Wilfrid Laurier Univ. Press.

Story of the hare. n.d. Sacred Texts. https://sacred-texts.com/afr/xft/xft25.htm

Strynatka, c. 2017. Religious Belief System of the Khoisans. Class Room.

https://classroom.synonym.com/hinduism-worship-of-the-sun-12087091.html

Swazi culture: The language, food and tradition of the Swati people. n.d. Answers Africa. https://answersafrica.com/swazi-culture-the-language-food-and-tradition-of-swati-people.html

The arrival of the Khoisan. 2020. SA History. https://www.sahistory.org.za/article/arrival-khoisan

The Batwa people. n.d. Bwinid Forest National Park. https://www.bwindiforestnationalpark.com/the-batwa-people.htm

The history of the San. n.d. Exploring Africa. https://www.exploring-africa.com/en/botswana/san-or-bushmen/history-san

The history of Vhavenda people. 2022. Opera News. https://za.opera.news/za/en/culture

The San. 2019. SA History. https://www.sahistory.org.za/article/san

Thembuland. n.d. SA History Online. https://www.sahistory.org.za/place/thembuland

Tietz, T. 2016. The Dscovery of the Tuang Child. Sci Hi Blog. http://scihi.org/discovery-taung-child/

Tsui-Goab. n.d. Tormento SA. http://tormentosa.co.za/Wiki/Topic.php/Spoiler/Tsui-Goab

Twice, N.P.K. 2021. The True History of Nguni People. NPK Twice. https://npktwice.wordpress.com/2021/08/18/the-true-history-of-nguni-people

Unkulunkulu. n.d. Gods of Creation. https://godsofcreation.weebly.com/unkulunkulu.html

Warten, W. 2019. Amapondo:Mpondo People. Blog Spot. https://mzansiyoutube.blogspot.com/2019/02/amampondo-mpondo-people.html

White, R. 2018. When and Why Did Our Human Ancestors First Leave Africa? UT News. https://news.utexas.edu/2018/07/11/when-and-why-did-our-human-ancestors-first-leave-africa/

Why do people form groups. 2020. Reference. https://www.reference.com/world-view/people-form-groups-8a80cb5051495940

Wilson, E, O. 2012. Biologist E.O. Wilson on Why Humans, Like Ants, Need a Tribe. News Week. https://www.newsweek.com/biologist-eo-wilson-why-humans-ants-need-tribe-64005

Written in the sand. n.d. Sassi. http://www.san.org.za/history.php

Xhosa. n.d. SA History Online. https://www.sahistory.org.za/article/xhosa

Yenhaka, M. n.d. A History of the Mutapa Empire. Tracks 4 Africa. https://media.tracks4africa.co.za/users/files/w314706_1651.pdf

Yong, E. 2016. Humans: Unusually Murderous Mammals, Typically Murderous Primates. The Atlantic. https://www.theatlantic.com/science/archive/2016/09/humans-

are-unusually-violent-mammals-but-averagely-violent-primates/501935/
Zulu folktales. n.d. S Life. https://slife.org/zulu-folktales
Zulu. n.d. South African History Online. https://www.sahistory.org.za/article/zulu
JAPANESE HISTORY: EXPLORE THE MAGNIFICENT HISTORY, CULTURE, MYTHOLOGY, FOLKLORE, WARS, LEGENDS, GREAT ACHIEVEMENTS & MORE OF JAPAN
Akatani, M. (2016). [The Cause of Death of Taira no Kiyomori: A Possible Connection with the Death of Fujiwara no Kunitsuna]. Nihon Ishigaku Zasshi. [Journal of Japanese History of Medicine], 62(1), 3–15. https://pubmed.ncbi.nlm.nih.gov/27464420/.
All Types of Japanese Swords (history and how they were used). (2020, August 29). Www.youtube.com. https://www.youtube.com/watch?v=oT8m3AOV_IY.
Axelrod, J. (2019). NPR Choice page. Npr.org. https://www.npr.org/sections/codeswitch/2019/08/11/742293305/a-century-later-the-treaty-of-versailles-and-its-rejection-of-racial-equality.
Commodore Perry and the Opening of Japan. (2021, February 7). Www.youtube.com. https://www.youtube.com/watch?v=MaZ95O6RmAc.
Emperor Go-Daigo. (2020, June 9). Wikipedia. https://en.wikipedia.org/wiki/Emperor_Go-Daigo.
Feature History. (2017). Feature History - Meiji Restoration. On YouTube. https://www.youtube.com/watch?v=Y_b58Rpg2YY.
History Summarized: The Meiji Restoration. (2020, May 8). Www.youtube.com. https://www.youtube.com/watch?v=Y5zlKYYp7bs.
How'd It Happen? History. (2017). What Happened to Japan after WW2? (How'd It Happen? History). In YouTube. https://www.youtube.com/watch?v=Lg4tQOEqU3o.
https://www.facebook.com/thoughtcodotcom. (2019). How to Be Beautiful in Heian Era Japan. ThoughtCo. https://www.thoughtco.com/beauty-in-heian-japan-195557.
Imperial Regalia of Japan. (2020, April 26). Wikipedia. https://en.wikipedia.org/wiki/Imperial_Regalia_of_Japan.
Izanagi. (2020, November 8). Wikipedia. https://en.wikipedia.org/wiki/Izanagi
Japan Omnibus - History - Early Japanese History. (2018). Japan-Zone.com. https://www.japan-zone.com/omnibus/history1.shtml.
Japanese history: Postwar. (2002, June 9). Japan-Guide.com. https://www.japan-guide.com/e/e2124.html.
Japanese Mythology - Myth Encyclopedia - god, story, legend, names, ancient, tree, famous, animal, world, Chinese. (2010).

Mythencyclopedia.com. http://www.mythencyclopedia.com/Iz-Le/Japanese-Mythology.html.

Kiger, P. J. (2019, September 20). 10 Inventions From China's Han Dynasty That Changed the World. HISTORY. https://www.history.com/news/han-dynasty-inventions.

Life in Edo Japan (1603-1868). (2019, April 27). Www.youtube.com. https://www.youtube.com/watch?v=wIygLo_W1Sw&t=456s.

Linfamy. (2019). Life of Early Japanese Women (So Much Cheating...) | History of Japan 38 [YouTube Video]. In YouTube. https://www.youtube.com/watch?v=Ylom3pm5SCo.

Minamoto no Yoritomo. (2020, March 11). Wikipedia. https://en.wikipedia.org/wiki/Minamoto_no_Yoritomo.

Mongol invasions of Japan. (2020, June 4). Wikipedia. https://en.wikipedia.org/wiki/Mongol_invasions_of_Japan.

Morison, S. E. (1967). Old Bruin Commodore Matthew C .perry 1794-1858. In Internet Archive. https://archive.org/stream/in.ernet.dli.2015.130945/2015.130945.Old-Bruin-Commodore-Methew-C-perry-1794-1858_djvu.txt.

Origins of the Yayoi people. (2008, June 27). Heritage of Japan. https://heritageofjapan.wordpress.com/yayoi-era-yields-up-rice/who-were-the-yayoi-people/.

Prehistory of Japan (Paleolithic, Jōmon and Yayoi periods). (n.d.). Www.youtube.com. Retrieved November 30, 2021, from https://www.youtube.com/watch?v=8Q4fRT081-0.

Proctor, M. (2015, June 25). Japanese Mythology: 5 Ancient Myths and Legends. TakeLessons Blog. https://takelessons.com/blog/japanese-mythology-z05.

Taika era reforms | Japanese history | Britannica. (2019). In Encyclopædia Britannica. https://www.britannica.com/event/Taika-era-reforms.

The Heian Period, an Age of Art...Ending in a Shogunate | History of Japan 34. (n.d.). Www.youtube.com. Retrieved December 2, 2021, from https://www.youtube.com/watch?v=9z8ZZezVmfw.

The Jomon, a 10,000 Year Old Culture (and Pots!) | History of Japan 3. (n.d.). Www.youtube.com. Retrieved November 30, 2021, from https://www.youtube.com/watch?v=gDBB5nazfM4.

The Rise of Japan: How did Japan become one of the World's Largest Economies? (2021, January 31). Www.youtube.com. https://www.youtube.com/watch?v=ytrpRLOaPzM

The Shogunate. (2019). The Samurai Tradition of Taking Heads. On YouTube. https://www.youtube.com/watch?v=TXPrkZ5Kpmo.

The Yayoi Arrive...and Change EVERYTHING! | History of Japan 4. (n.d.). Www.youtube.com. https://www.youtube.com/watch?v=bDnV9UvrpaU&t=5s.

Truman Statement on Hiroshima. (n.d.). Atomic Heritage Foundation. https://www.atomicheritage.org/key-documents/truman-statement-

hiroshima#:~:text=If%20they%20do%20not%20now.
Volcanoes of Japan: facts & information / VolcanoDiscovery. (2020). Volcanodiscovery.com. https://www.volcanodiscovery.com/japan.html.
W, S. (2013, November 8). The Ainu. Tofugu. https://www.tofugu.com/japan/ainu-japan/
Warring States Japan: Sengoku Jidai - Battle of Okehazama - Extra History - #1. (2014, November 8). Www.youtube.com. https://www.youtube.com/watch?v=hDsdkoln59A&list=PLhyKYa0YJ_5A649vEQk37316BH8FsaU24.
Warring States Japan: Sengoku Jidai - How Toyotomi Unified Japan - Extra History - #5. (2015, January 17). Www.youtube.com. https://www.youtube.com/watch?v=lBD8OAegEw0&list=PLhyKYa0YJ_5A649vEQk37316BH8FsaU24&index=5.
Warring States Japan: Sengoku Jidai - The Campaign of Sekigahara - Extra History - #6. (2015, January 31). Www.youtube.com. https://www.youtube.com/watch?v=5vscOHPFUf0&list=PLhyKYa0YJ_5A649vEQk37316BH8FsaU24&index=6.
Warring States Japan: Sengoku Jidai - The Death of Oda Nobunaga - Extra History - #4. (2014, December 20). Www.youtube.com. https://www.youtube.com/watch?v=ht6h4-MsMOY&list=PLhyKYa0YJ_5A649vEQk37316BH8FsaU24&index=4.
Warring States Japan: Sengoku Jidai - The Siege of Inabayama Castle - Extra History - #2. (2014, November 22). Www.youtube.com. https://www.youtube.com/watch?v=I2yT2nitGDk&list=PLhyKYa0YJ_5A649vEQk37316BH8FsaU24&index=2.
Warring States Japan: Sengoku Jidai - Warrior Monks of Hongan-ji and Hiei - Extra History - #3. (2014, December 6). Www.youtube.com. https://www.youtube.com/watch?v=G3frtoMaxZE&list=PLhyKYa0YJ_5A649vEQk37316BH8FsaU24&index=3.
Why Japan Got off Easy in WW2 - The HORRIBLE Atrocities of the Japanese Empire. (2021, June 6). Www.youtube.com. http://youtube.com/watch?v=uBEmMeZOYaI.
Wikipedia Contributors. (2019a, March 12). Genpei War. Wikipedia; Wikimedia Foundation. https://en.wikipedia.org/wiki/Genpei_War.
Wikipedia Contributors. (2019b, July 3). Nara period. Wikipedia; Wikimedia Foundation. https://en.wikipedia.org/wiki/Nara_period.
Wikipedia Contributors. (2019c, September 14). Sengoku period. Wikipedia; Wikimedia Foundation. https://en.wikipedia.org/wiki/Sengoku_period.
Wikipedia Contributors. (2021a, April 18). Ōnin War. Wikipedia; Wikimedia Foundation. https://en.wikipedia.org/wiki/%C5%8Cnin_War.
Wikipedia Contributors. (2021b, August 12). Dōkyō. Wikipedia;

Wikimedia Foundation. https://en.wikipedia.org/wiki/D%C5%8Dky%C5%8D.
Wikipedia Contributors. (2021c, October 27). Jōkyū War. Wikipedia; Wikimedia Foundation. https://en.wikipedia.org/wiki/J%C5%8Dky%C5%AB_War.
WorldAtlas. (2019, January 18). Why Is Volcanic Soil Fertile? WorldAtlas. https://www.worldatlas.com/articles/why-is-volcanic-soil-fertile.html.

HOODOO FOR BEGINNERS: CONNECT TO THE ANCIENT SPIRIT WORLD OF AFRICA & MANIFEST SUCCESS WITH SPELLS, ROOT MAGIC, CONJURING, HERBS, TRADITIONS, HISTORY & MORE

African Diaspora Cultures | Oldways. (2019). Oldways. https://oldwayspt.org/traditional-diets/african-heritage-diet/african-diaspora-cultures

Alvarado, D. (2009). The Voodoo Hoodoo Spellbook. In Google Books. Lulu.com. https://books.google.lk/books?id=ia1BAgAAQBAJ&pg=PA115&lpg=PA115&dq=hoodoo+talismans&source=bl&ots=ptMr55jafw&sig=ACfU3U0_x6tnJcUrEu3Zex1_IP4m-vC4uw&hl=en&sa=X&ved=2ahUKEwizmcKU09b3AhXh7XMBHbS7BR0Q6AF6BAgfEAM#v=onepage&q=hoodoo%20talismans&f=false

Anderson, J. E. (2005). Conjure in African American Society. In Google Books. LSU Press. https://books.google.lk/books?hl=en&lr=&id=9sR_6jhCRN0C&oi=fnd&pg=PR9&ots=rZVTDgKW2g&sig=6r09fo42QAWvwe_-IoW28Egud2E&redir_esc=y#v=onepage&q&f=false

Asante, M., & Mazama, A. (2009). Mawu-Lisa. SAGE Knowledge; SAGE Publications, Inc. https://sk.sagepub.com/reference/africanreligion/n259.xml

Beck, J. J. (2006). Root Doctors | NCpedia. Www.ncpedia.org. https://www.ncpedia.org/root-doctors

Chireau, Y. P. (2003). Black Magic: Religion and the African American Conjuring Tradition. In Google Books. University of California Press. https://books.google.lk/books?hl=en&lr=&id=-BuLuB6sZ_kC&oi=fnd&pg=PA1&ots=aZLSYVlCY4&sig=yMQoruuYsTEbpyUdmMoxGJk9jbU&redir_esc=y#v=onepage&q&f=false

Conjure Oils, Hoodoo Oils, Ritual Oils, Dressing Oils, and Anointing Oils for Hoodoo Rootwork and Magic Spells. (n.d.). Www.luckymojo.com. Retrieved May 6, 2022, from https://www.luckymojo.com/oils.html

Cordin, E. (2022, May 6). How To Cast A Love Spell [Updated Guide 2022]. The Island Now. https://theislandnow.com/blog-112/how-to-cast-a-love-spell/

Crystals, A. H. (2019, November). Introduction to Hoodoo Magic with Crystals. AtPerry's Healing Crystals. https://shop.atperrys.com/blogs/healing-crystals-blog/introduction-to-hoodoo-magic-with-crystals#toc_1

Definition of MAGICO-RELIGIOUS. (n.d.). Www.merriam-Webster.com. Retrieved May 2, 2022, from https://www.merriam-webster.com/dictionary/magico-religious

Ernst, M. (2014, January). Witch 101: Graveyard Etiquette. Crystal Crush Magazine. https://www.crystalcrushmagazine.com/magick/1-7-2021/ibphmpcgcpdi30dip54e1e5sifbcgw

Ethnicity Facts for Benin & Togo - AncestryDNA. (n.d.). Www.ancestry.com. https://www.ancestry.com/dna/ethnicity/benin-togo

Five Finger Grass. (n.d.). Freya's Cauldron. Retrieved May 9, 2022, from https://www.freyascauldron.com/ourshop/prod_6346329-Five-Finger-Grass.html

Fon | people. (n.d.). Encyclopedia Britannica. https://www.britannica.com/topic/Fon-people

Haitian Vodou. (2022, April 15). Wikipedia. https://en.wikipedia.org/wiki/Haitian_Vodou#The_nanchon

Hauser, W., Hansen, E., & Enck, P. (n.d.). Deutsches Ärzteblatt: Archiv "Nocebo Phenomena in Medicine" (29.06.2012). Www.aerzteblatt.de. https://www.aerzteblatt.de/pdf.asp?id=127210

Hawkins, D. A. (2021, January). Why some young Black Christians are practicing hoodoo. The Christian Century. https://www.christiancentury.org/article/features/why-some-young-black-christians-are-practicing-hoodoo

Hoodoo (folk magic). (n.d.). Religion Wiki. Retrieved May 6, 2022, from https://religion.fandom.com/wiki/Hoodoo_(folk_magic)#Hoodoo_conceptual_system

Hoodoo in St. Louis: An African American Religious Tradition (U.S. National Park Service). (n.d.). Www.nps.gov. https://www.nps.gov/articles/000/hoodoo-in-st-louis-an-african-american-religious-tradition.htm

Hoodoo: Black Magic or Healing Art? (n.d.). https://english.cofc.edu/first-year-writing/Hoodoo%20Healing%20Art.pdf

Humpálová, D. (2012). Západočeská univerzita v Plzni Fakulta filozofická Bakalářská práce VOODOO IN LOUISIANA. https://core.ac.uk/download/pdf/295552849.pdf

Incense. (n.d.). AromaG's Botanica. Retrieved May 11, 2022, from https://www.aromagregory.com/esoteric-goods/incense/

Lane, M. (2005). HOODOO HERITAGE: A BRIEF HISTORY OF AMERICAN FOLK RELIGION. https://getd.libs.uga.edu/pdfs/lane_megan_e_200805_ma.pdf

Lucky W Amulet Archive: Good Luck Charms, Magic Talismans, Protection Amulets. (n.d.). Www.luckymojo.com. Retrieved May 6, 2022, from https://www.luckymojo.com/saintexpedite.html

Magic Herbs, Roots, Mineral Curios: Lucky Mojo Curio Co. Catalogue. (n.d.). Www.luckymojo.com. Retrieved May 6, 2022, from https://www.luckymojo.com/mojocatherbs.html#special

Manbo (Vodou). (2022, April 1). Wikipedia. https://en.wikipedia.org/wiki/Manbo_(Vodou)#Vodou_priesthood

Moose, H. S. (n.d.). Working Conjure: A Guide to Hoodoo Folk Magic (Paperback) | Politics and Prose Bookstore. Www.politics-Prose.com. https://www.politics-prose.com/book/9781578636273

Oxford Reference. (n.d.). https://www.oxfordreference.com/view/10.1093/oi/authority.20110803095936832

PeopleLife. (2022, February 3). Why do Native Americans burn incense? Flashmode Magazine | Magazine de Mode et Style de Vie Numéro Un En Tunisie et Au Maghreb. https://flashmode.tn/magazine/why-do-native-americans-burn-incense/

Pfingsten, M., Leibing, E., Harter, W., Kröner-Herwig, B., Hempel, D., Kronshage, U., & Hildebrandt, J. (2001). Fear-Avoidance Behavior and Anticipation of Pain in Patients With Chronic Low Back Pain: A Randomized Controlled Study. Pain Medicine, 2(4), 259–266. https://doi.org/10.1046/j.1526-4637.2001.01044.x

PlaceboEffect. (2021, May). Frontiers in Behavioral Science. https://www.frontiersin.org/articles/10.3389/fnbeh.2021.653359/full

Psalm 51. (n.d.). Psalm 51 KJV - - Bible Gateway. Www.biblegateway.com. https://www.biblegateway.com/passage/?search=Psalm%2051&version=KJV

Psalm108. (n.d.). Bible Gateway passage: Psalm 108 - King James Version. Bible Gateway. Retrieved May 11, 2022, from https://www.biblegateway.com/passage/?search=Psalm+108&version=KJV

Psalm118. (n.d.). Bible Gateway passage: Psalm 118 - King James Version. Bible Gateway. Retrieved May 11, 2022, from https://www.biblegateway.com/passage/?search=Psalm+118&version=KJV

Pslam91. (n.d.). Bible Gateway Psalm 91 :: NIV. Web.mit.edu. Retrieved May 11, 2022, from https://web.mit.edu/jywang/www/cef/Bible/NIV/NIV_Bible/PS+91.html

Pslam91. (2015). Bible Gateway passage: Psalm 91 - King James Version.

Bible Gateway; BibleGateway. https://www.biblegateway.com/passage/?search=Psalm+91&version=KJV

Robinson, C. (2021). Hoodoo For Beginners: An Introduction to African American Folk Magic. In Google Books. Creek Ridge Publishing. https://books.google.lk/books?hl=en&lr=&id=0Wc9EAAAQBAJ&oi=fnd&pg=PA1&dq=cemetery+hoodoo&ots=xKyk9YXa4Q&sig=7uYrMAgAPUH1g4csJ54idqMSPUA&redir_esc=y#v=onepage&q=cemetery%20hoodoo&f=false

Shurpin, Y. (n.d.). Chad.org. https://www.chabad.org/library/article_cdo/aid/4064052/jewish/Why-Wash-Hands-After-a-Funeral-or-Cemetery-Visit.htm

Slavery - Slavery in the Americas | Britannica. (2019). In Encyclopædia Britannica. https://www.britannica.com/topic/slavery-sociology/Slavery-in-the-Americas

The Benefits of Florida Water. (2020, August 30). Hoodoo Magic Spells. https://hoodoomagicspells.com/the-benefits-of-florida-water/

The Editors of Encyclopedia Britannica. (2015). Dahomey | historical kingdom, Africa. In Encyclopædia Britannica. https://www.britannica.com/place/Dahomey-historical-kingdom-Africa

Universe, V. (2021, August 24). HooDoo How We Do: Angelica Root For Plagues and Protection. Voodoo Universe. https://www.patheos.com/blogs/voodoouniverse/2021/08/hoodoo-how-we-do-angelica-root-for-plagues-and-protection/

Vandal root - Valerian. (n.d.). AromaG's Botanica. Retrieved May 9, 2022, from https://www.aromagregory.com/product/vandal-root-valerian/

Video: Black Magic Matters: Hoodoo as Ancestral Religion. (2021, December). Cswr.hds.harvard.edu. https://cswr.hds.harvard.edu/news/magic-matters/2021/11/10

Vodou, Not "Voodoo." (2010, February). Journal Times. https://journaltimes.com/vodou-not-voodoo/article_62bcf36a-1816-11df-89c6-001cc4c03286.html

VodouOrVoodoo. (n.d.). Family helps adopted Haitian children keep their spiritual heritage. Www.vcstar.com. Retrieved April 30, 2022, from https://archive.vcstar.com/lifestyle/family-helps-adopted-haitian-children-keep-their-spiritual-heritage-ep-369779629-350144391.html

Wonders of the African World - Episodes - Slave Kingdoms - Wonders. (n.d.). Www.pbs.org. Retrieved April 29, 2022, from https://www.pbs.org/wonders/Episodes/Epi3/3_wondr3.htm

Woody, B. (2019). The American Crusades: Exploring the Impact of Marine Persecution of Vodou in U.S. Occupied Haiti. Historical Perspectives: Santa Clara University Undergraduate Journal of

History, Series II, 23. https://scholarcommons.scu.edu/cgi/viewcontent.cgi?article=1165&context=historical-perspectives

World Health Organization. (2021). Obesity and overweight. World Health Organization. https://www.who.int/news-room/fact-sheets/detail/obesity-and-overweight

OTHER BOOKS BY HISTORY BROUGHT ALIVE

- Ancient Egypt: Discover Fascinating History, Mythology, Gods, Goddesses, Pharaohs, Pyramids, and More from the Mysterious Ancient Egyptian Civilization.

Available now on Kindle, Paperback, Hardcover & Audio in all regions

- Greek Mythology: Explore The Timeless Tales Of Ancient Greece, The Myths, History & Legends of The Gods, Goddesses, Titans, Heroes, Monsters & More

Available now on Kindle, Paperback, Hardcover & Audio in all regions

- Mythology for Kids: Explore Timeless Tales, Characters, History, & Legendary Stories from Around the World. Norse, Celtic, Roman, Greek, Egypt & Many More

Available now on Kindle, Paperback, Hardcover & Audio in all regions

- Mythology of Mesopotamia: Fascinating Insights, Myths, Stories & History From The World's Most Ancient Civilization. Sumerian, Akkadian, Babylonian, Persian, Assyrian and More

Available now on Kindle, Paperback, Hardcover & Audio in all regions

- Norse Magic & Runes: A Guide To The Magic, Rituals, Spells & Meanings of Norse Magick, Mythology & Reading The Elder Futhark Runes

Available now on Kindle, Paperback, Hardcover & Audio in all regions

- Norse Mythology, Vikings, Magic & Runes: Stories, Legends & Timeless Tales From Norse & Viking Folklore + A Guide To The Rituals, Spells & Meanings of Norse Magick & The Elder Futhark Runes. (3 books in 1)

Available now on Kindle, Paperback, Hardcover & Audio in all regions

- Norse Mythology: Captivating Stories & Timeless Tales Of Norse Folklore. The Myths, Sagas & Legends of The Gods, Immortals, Magical Creatures, Vikings & More

Available now on Kindle, Paperback, Hardcover & Audio in all regions

- Norse Mythology for Kids: Legendary Stories, Quests & Timeless Tales from Norse Folklore. The Myths, Sagas & Epics of the Gods, Immortals, Magic Creatures, Vikings & More

Available now on Kindle, Paperback, Hardcover & Audio in all regions

- Roman Empire: Rise & The Fall. Explore The History, Mythology, Legends, Epic Battles & Lives Of The Emperors, Legions, Heroes, Gladiators & More

Available now on Kindle, Paperback, Hardcover & Audio in all regions

- The Vikings: Who Were The Vikings? Enter The Viking Age & Discover The Facts, Sagas, Norse Mythology, Legends, Battles & More

Available now on Kindle, Paperback, Hardcover & Audio in all regions

- Hoodoo for Beginners: Connect to the Ancient Spirit World of Africa & Manifest Success with Spells, Root Magic, Conjuring, Herbs, Traditions, History & More

Available now on Kindle, Paperback, Hardcover & Audio in all regions

- Native American History: Accurate & Comprehensive History, Origins, Culture, Tribes, Legends, Mythology, Wars, Stories & More of the Native Indigenous Americans

Available now on Kindle, Paperback, Hardcover & Audio in all regions

- Norse Mythology Legends: Epic Stories, Quests, Myths & More from the Most Powerful Characters, Gods, Goddesses & Heroes of Norse & Viking Folklore

Available now on Kindle, Paperback, Hardcover & Audio in all regions

- African History: Explore the Amazing Timeline of the World's Richest Continent—The History, Culture, Folklore, Mythology & More of Africa

Available now on Kindle, Paperback, Hardcover & Audio in all regions

- The History of China: A Concise Introduction to Chinese History, Culture, Dynasties, Mythology, Great Achievements & More of the Oldest Living Civilization

Available now on Kindle, Paperback, Hardcover & Audio in all regions

- History of Asia: Explore the Magnificent Histories, Culture, Mythology, Folklore, Wars, Legends, Stories, Achievements & More of China, Japan & India: 3 Books in

1

Available now on Kindle, Paperback, Hardcover & Audio in all regions

- Norse Mythology, Vikings, Magic & Runes: Stories, Legends & Timeless Tales from Norse & Viking Folklore + A Guide to the Rituals, Spells & Meanings of ... Elder Futhark Runes: 3 Books (3 Books in 1)

Available now on Kindle, Paperback, Hardcover & Audio in all regions

- Norse Paganism for Beginners: Explore the History of the Old Norse Religion: Asatru, Cosmology, Astrology, Mythology, Magic, Runes, Tarot, Witchcraft & More

Available now on Kindle, Paperback, Hardcover & Audio in all regions

- Greek, Mesopotamia, Egypt, and Rome: Fascinating Insights, Mythology, Stories, History, and Knowledge from the World's Most Interesting Civilizations and Empires: 4 books in 1

Available now on Kindle, Paperback, Hardcover & Audio in all regions

- Mythology of Mesopotamia: Fascinating Insights, Myths, Stories & History From the World's Most Ancient Civilization. Sumerian, Akkadian, Babylonian, Persian, Assyrian and More

Available now on Kindle, Paperback, Hardcover & Audio in all regions

- Japanese History: Explore the Magnificent History, Culture, Mythology, Folklore, Wars, Legends, Great

Achievements & More of Japan

Available now on Kindle, Paperback, Hardcover & Audio in all regions

- History of India: A Concise Introduction to Indian History, Culture, Mythology, Religion, Gandhi, Characters, Empires, Achievements & More Throughout the Ages

Available now on Kindle, Paperback, Hardcover & Audio in all regions

- Greek Mythology for Kids: Explore Timeless Tales & Bedtime Stories from Ancient Greece. Myths, History, Fantasy & Adventures of the Gods, Goddesses, Titans, Heroes, Monsters & More

Available now on Kindle, Paperback, Hardcover & Audio in all regions

- Egyptian Mythology for Kids: Discover Fascinating History, Facts, Gods, Goddesses, Bedtime Stories, Pharaohs, Pyramids, Mummies & More from Ancient Egypt

Available now on Kindle, Paperback, Hardcover & Audio in all regions

FREE BONUS FROM HBA: EBOOK BUNDLE

Greetings!

First of all, thank you for reading our books. As fellow passionate readers of History and Mythology, we aim to create the very best books for our readers.

Now, we invite you to join our VIP list. As a welcome gift, we offer the History & Mythology Ebook Bundle below for free. Plus you can be the first to receive new books and exclusives! Remember it's 100% free to join.

Scan the QR code to join.

AFRICAN HISTORY & HOODOO

We sincerely hope you enjoyed our new book "**AFRICAN HISTORY & HOODOO**". We would greatly appreciate your feedback with an honest review at the place of purchase.

First and foremost, we are always looking to grow and improve as a team. It is reassuring to hear what works, as well as receive constructive feedback on what should improve. Second, starting out as an unknown author is exceedingly difficult, and Amazon reviews go a long way toward making the journey out of anonymity possible. Please take a few minutes to write an honest review.

Best regards,

History Brought Alive

http://historybroughtalive.com/